JOINT FORCES STAFF COLLEGE

Two Independent Pillars of Policy- The Saudi and American Approaches to Iran

04 April 2008

This Page Intentionally Left Blank

Abstract

With the 2003 invasion of Iraq and subsequent instability in Iraq, the Kingdom of Saudi Arabia and the Islamic Republic of Iran find themselves at the center of a struggle for power in the Middle East. The Sunni-dominant Kingdom, with its oil wealth, religious and cultural importance, and Arab voice, competes in a battle to increase soft power influence against the Shiite-dominant Islamic Republic, a nation, strengthened by the collapse of the Hussein, seeking to regain its empirical past.

Iran seeks to build its power base through lending support to particular factions in regional struggles. Additionally, others argue that Iran is pursuing a nuclear weapons capability not only to deter aggressors but to gain status in the international community. In response to these behaviors, Saudi Arabia remains actively engaged in the region to counterbalance the growth of Iranian influence. Concerned with the stability of the Middle East, the United States continues to implement the remaining half of the dual containment policy initiated by President Clinton, despite conflicting evidence of its true effectiveness.

While the motivations of the U.S. and the Kingdom may differ, their dissimilar methods to reduce the influence of Iran are necessary. Two pillars of effort, one at the international level headed by the U.S. and one at the regional level executed by Saudi Arabia, both acting independently, may effectively marginalize Iran as a threat.

This thesis identifies the appropriateness of the Saudi approach to handling Iran from a regional perspective and challenges the relevancy of the current U.S. foreign policy, advocating alternative unilateral and multilateral efforts.

This Page Intentionally Left Blank

CONTENTS

TABLES

Chapter One

1. INTRODUCTION

Tension permeates throughout the Middle East. The themes that define this tension vary throughout the region. Sometimes territorial, sometimes cultural, and yet sometimes sectarian, the disputes have existed since the nascent years of most of these Middle Eastern countries. Regional alliances, cooperation, and friendships have fluctuated dramatically in the past century, particularly with the fall of the Saddam Hussein regime in Iraq. Two predominant nations, the Kingdom of Saudi Arabia and the Islamic Republic of Iran are now redefining the regional environment in which they will co-exist.

Undeniably, Iran is aggressively seeking to expand its sphere of influence with the fall of the Saddam Hussein regime in Iraq. Its methods are unconventional yet effective. For example, sponsorship of Islamic extremist organizations, whether it is in Palestine or Iraq, disrupts any progress of stability or peace in these areas. Although Iran has claimed to have abandoned its goal of spreading Shiite power to the southern Gulf States, its behavior invokes the opposite. The rhetoric of its President, Mahmud Ahmadinejad, openly expresses a desire for a Shiite crescent, raising much concern from its Sunni neighbors.[1]

Saudi Arabia, a predominant Sunni community that is no longer an impoverished, insular state but rather a regional player,[2] foresees the threat of Iran's Islamic revolution penetrating the Arabian Peninsula, with the fall of a strong buffer provided by Iraq.

---

[1] Anthony H. Cordesman and Khalid R. Al-Rodhan, *Gulf Military Forces in an Era of Asymmetric Wars* (Westport, Connecticut: Praeger Security International, 2007), 319.

[2] Rachel Bronson, *Thicker Than Oil—America's Uneasy Partnership with Saudi Arabia* (New York: Oxford University Press, 2006), 7.

Saudi Arabia is a state whose domestic troubles threaten its own internal stability, and who now finds itself, the longstanding unofficial leader of the Arab nations, in the forefront of all the Gulf States to maintain some relative regional peace with Iran. The Saudi royal family, in multiple policy dimensions, seeks to marginalize the influence of Iran. In the backdrop of all its actions, the Kingdom remains cautious that the threat of Iran is a threat from another Muslim state. Thus, unless openly attacked by Iran, Saudi Arabia's self-protection policy measures must appear transparent and unaggressive. The Kingdom's direct and indirect methods to diplomatically and economically shape the regional environment compel Iran to recognize the importance of engagement with its Arab neighbor.

Contrary to the Saudi approach, policy taken by the President of the United States with regards to the regime in Tehran is firm and direct. George W. Bush's foreign policy eventually led to the removal of the tyrannical ruler of Saddam Hussein in Iraq and the stern rhetoric towards Iran suggests a similar end to its existing government in the eyes of the Middle East. More U.S. military force in the region will reinforce the Muslim view of a Western invasion by an infidel, and thus, support from Arab nations like Saudi Arabia of such an aggressive stance remain distant. The most significant measures by the Bush administration include sanctions which seek to isolate Iran, an alternative that analysts offer both approval and disagreement. All attempts to single out and isolate the Islamic Republic of Iran seem ineffective. Rather than being an intimidated nation, Iran continues to be determined to set its own agenda.

Thesis Statement

While the motivations of the United States and Saudi Arabia may differ, their dissimilar methods to reduce the influence of the Islamic Republic of Iran are necessary. Two pillars of effort, one at the international level executed by the U.S. and one at the regional level executed by the Kingdom of Saudi Arabia, both acting independently, may effectively marginalize the threat that Iran poses to both nations. The Saudi Arabian approach is regionally appropriate, and with the U.S. as a prominent international figure consistently seeking to gain an effective approach of its own, Iran may indeed find greater difficulty in creating or maintaining the rise of its Islamic revolution and in pursuing its right as a legitimate state within the region.

This thesis examines the current standing and strategic importance of the two regional rivals—the Kingdom of Saudi Arabia and the Islamic Republic of Iran—and outlines the recent foreign policy measures of the Kingdom and the U.S. with respect to Iran. After an evaluation of both from the regional and international perspectives, the thesis offers a U.S. policy alternative that may generate more favorable relations with Iran and evaluates the necessity of linking the two approaches to reducing the rising Iranian influence.

Chapter Two

2. AN OVERVIEW OF THE KINGDOM OF SAUDI ARABIA

It is critical to examine particular aspects of Saudi Arabia to discern the rationale taken by the Saudi leadership with regards to their foreign policy with Iran. In general, Saudi Arabia, a country of abundant energy resources and a central religious and cultural figure, lacks the military dimension needed to effectively counter a regional threat.

The Kingdom of Saudi Arabia— ITS IMPORTANCE

Geographical Significance

"The Kingdom of Saudi Arabia is the largest and most powerful state in the Arabian Peninsula."[1] Strategically centered in the Middle East, it is the biggest country in the Gulf and one of the largest in the Middle East, amassing 1,960,582 square kilometers, compared to Iran's 1,648,000 square kilometers. Saudi Arabia borders every country in the Gulf except Iran and has a coastline of 2,640 kilometers with access to two absolutely critical Middle Eastern sea lanes: 1,840 kilometers on the Red Sea and 700 kilometers on the Persian Gulf. With these coastlines, Saudi Arabia may leverage the shipping of international trade through the Suez Canal, the Strait of Hormuz and Bab el-Mandeb.[2] Its geographical dominance in the Arabian Peninsula captures the attention of any legitimate regional actor.

Resource Significance

The Kingdom is also synonymous with oil, as the nation with the largest oil reserves (260 billion barrels or 25% of the world's known reserves) and the largest oil

---

[1] J.E. Peterson, "Saudi Arabia and the Illusion of Security," *Adelphi Paper 348* (July 2002): 7.

[2] Cordesman and Al-Rodhan, 163.

producing capacity in the world. The figure below offers international comparison to some of its contemporaries:

TOP 10 COUNTRIES IN THE WORLD IN 2006 (thousand barrels per day)											
OIL PRODUCERS			**OIL CONSUMERS**			**OIL NET IMPORTERS**			**OIL NET EXPORTERS**		
1	Saudi Arabia	10,665	1	U.S.	20,687	1	U.S.	12,357	1	Saudi Arabia	8,525
2	Russia	9,677	2	China	7,273	2	Japan	5,031	2	Russia	6,816
3	U.S.	8,330	3	Japan	5,159	3	China	3,428	3	UAE	2,564
4	Iran	4,148	4	Russia	2,861	4	Germany	2,514	4	Norway	2,551
5	China	3,845	5	Germany	2,665	5	South Korea	2,156	5	Iran	2,462
6	Mexico	3,707	6	India	2,587	6	France	1,890	6	Kuwait	2,342
7	Canada	3,288	7	Canada	2,264	7	India	1,733	7	Venezuela	2,183
8	UAE	2,945	8	Brazil	2,217	8	Italy	1,568	8	Nigeria	2,131
9	Venezuela	2,803	9	South Korea	2,174	9	Spain	1,562	9	Algeria	1,842
10	Norway	2,786	10	Mexico	2,139	10	Taiwan	940	10	Mexico	1,710

Figure 2.1: 2006 Comparative Oil Statistics[3]

Historically maintaining 12.5% of world total production for the last ten years, Saudi Arabia also has approximately 1.5-2.0 million barrels per day of spare capacity and predicts to have a 15 million barrel per day production capability within the next 15 years.[4] Of all the oil producing nations, Saudi Arabia clearly has the most unique capability of bearing the cost of maintaining spare oil capacity. With the ability to put oil onto the market in times of crisis, holding around 85 percent of the Organization of Petroleum Exporting Countries' (OPEC) spare capacity, the Kingdom can singularly impact the international community.[5] OPEC currently consists of thirteen nations which include Iran, Iraq, Kuwait, Qatar, Saudi Arabia, the United Arab Emirates (UAE),

---

[3] U.S. Department of Energy, Energy Information Administration, *Country Energy Profiles,* 2006, http://tonto.eia.doe.gov/country/index.cfm (accessed March 6, 2008).

[4] Cordesman and Al-Rodhan, 165.

[5] Rachel Bronson, *Thicker Than Oil* (New York: Oxford University Press, 2006), 22.

Venezuela, Algeria, Angola, Ecuador, Indonesia, Libya, and Qatar.[6] And so, when another big producer suffers a decline in production, such as Iraq descending into chaos or U.S. oil facilities suffering damages due to hurricanes, Saudi Arabia may quickly make up the volumes.[7] Due to the Kingdom's indigenous resources, it can significantly impact the petroleum based economies of other states.

Cultural Significance

Beyond all the petroleum, Saudi Arabia is also the location of the two holiest places in Islam and the Center of the Pilgrimage. As a result, the Kingdom routinely has the opportunity to advance its interests to the millions of Muslims that come to participate in the hajj. As the custodian of the two most important shrines in Islam and empowered by oil wealth, Saudi Arabia is the crucial member that sets the tone for Middle Eastern policies and attitudes in organizations such as the Arab League, which includes the Organization of Islamic Conference, and the Gulf Cooperation Council (GCC), which includes Bahrain, Kuwait, Oman, and Qatar.[8]

The Sunni population dominates the Kingdom at 85 to 90% of the total Saudi population of 22 million in 2007,[9] with the remaining 10% to 15% being Shiite.[10] "The Shiite-Sunni rift has been a major pillar in determining the balance of power in the region

---

[6] Organization of the Petroleum Exporting Countries, "Who are OPEC Member Countries?" Organization of the Petroleum Exporting Countries, http://www.opec.org/library/FAQs/aboutOPEC/q3.htm (accessed January 27, 2008).

[7] Bronson, 22.

[8] Cordesman and Al-Rodhan, 163-164.

[9] U.S. Department of State, Bureau of Near Eastern Affairs, *Background Note: Saudi Arabia,* February 2008, http://www.state.gov/r/pa/ei/bgn/3584.htm (accessed January 6, 2008).

[10] Febe Armanios, "Islam: Sunnis and Shiite," Congressional Research Service, February 23, 2005.

since the Shiite split from Sunni Islam in A.D. 680. . . From a strategic and security point of view, it (determining the balance of power) is a question of demographics. As has been all too clear in the case of Iraq, the sectarian compositions of countries determine alliances, influence the political dynamics of each country, and impact internal security."[11] These demographics shape much of the Kingdom's policy to favor this community. However, the minority sect of the Shiites does occupy the oil rich Eastern Province of the Kingdom.[12]

Political Reform

Since the Kingdom was first established in the early 19th century, the union of Wahhabi fundamentalism and the House of Saud authority was the source of its strict conservative government. As a monarchy with a Council of Ministers and a Consultative Council which are guided by the Holy Qur'an, Shari'a and the Basic Law, the Kingdom has no political parties, with the executive chief of state and head of government being the King and the advisory body being the legislative Consultative Council.[13] However, with the events of September 11, 2001, the Kingdom re-examined and somewhat reformed its government structure. King Abdullah bin Abdulaziz, pursued various reform initiatives in the summer of 2003 that clashed with the traditionalist elements of Saudi society. The initiatives created conditions whereby "Within less than a year three demarcation lines' were cut across with the support of the Crown Prince—the sectarian line, the regional line and the sexual line—suffusing the process of Saudi nation building

---

[11] Cordesman and Al-Rodhan, 261.

[12] Cordesman and Al-Rodhan, 408.

[13] U.S. Department of State, Bureau of Near Eastern Affairs, *Background Note: Saudi Arabia,* February 2008, http://www.state.gov/r/pa/ei/bgn/3584.htm (accessed January 6, 2008).

with new energy."[14] By advocating dialogue throughout the Kingdom and promoting a

supervised and limited form of political participation, King Abdullah has set the nation in

a general direction of gradual change. The people are beginning to no longer define

themselves as belonging to the Wahhabi community, but increasingly as citizens of the

Saudi state. But while the conservative ulama may altogether become insignificant over

time, the nation proceeds with caution and the rulers will stop the process whenever it

threatens to get out of control.[15] Nevertheless, the royal family recognizes the need to

change to a more inclusive government, evident in its gradual acceptance of more

representation.

The Kingdom of Saudi Arabia— ITS MILITARY CAPABILITY

As the Kingdom addresses the growing sentiment for political reform, Saudi

Arabia must still maintain a military that acknowledges the full spectrum of security

threats. The Kingdom's geographical boundaries compel it to deploy the military to

cover border nations such as Iraq, Jordan, and Syria, simultaneously defending the coasts

of the Red Sea and the Persian Gulf. With so many neighboring nations, Saudi Arabia

must normally disperse its forces. It must also address the current threat from internal

and external Islamic extremists, and not just from regular armies, navies, and air forces.[16]

In general, the Kingdom's military might maintains a diverse capability and a large pool

of military servicemen, and seeks to keep pace with its contemporaries. However, an

expert in the Middle East region such as Anthony H. Cordesman may argue that despite

---

[14] Paul Aarts and Gerd Nonneman, *Saudi Arabia in the Balance: Political Economy, Society, Foreign Affairs* (New York: New York University Press, 2005), 227

[15] Aarts and Nonneman, 231-233.

[16] Cordesman and Al-Rodhan, 166.

the technological capabilities of its military, the Kingdom is unable to train and maintain its military to address the nation's regional challenges without assistance from other nations.

Saudi Military Composition

The current Saudi security apparatus that must deal with this mix of strategic threats and pressures is a complex mix of regular military forces in the Ministry of Defense and Aviation (MODA), a separate Saudi Arabian National Guard (SANG), and various internal security and intelligence services in the Ministry of Interior (MOI). Saudi Arabia's military forces are only one element of the Saudi security structure and are currently divided into five major branches: the army, the national guard, the navy, the air force, and the air defense force. Saudi Arabia also has large paramilitary and internal security forces and a small strategic missile force.[17]

Saudi Defense Foreign Expenditures

The Kingdom's military structure has historically relied heavily upon the purchase of equipment from foreign military industry. U.S. reports on Saudi military and security spending estimate that Saudi security expenditures have generally been extremely high. The International Institute of Strategic Studies (IISS) uses unclassified Saudi budget data to calculate the total Saudi security budget, including internal security and estimates that from 2001 to 2004. According to their analysis, the Kingdom has used between 33% to 37% of its total budget on military and security spending in response to the growth of manpower, concentrating on the creation of infrastructure, foreign services and maintenance, and basic manpower training.[18] Expenditures of this magnitude demonstrate a continued intent to increase its capability to defend its borders.

---

[17] Cordesman and Al-Rodhan, 168.

[18] Cordesman and Al-Rodhan, 174-175.

Saudi Arms Imports

The Saudi security apparatus is very dependent on other nations for virtually all of its arms and military technology. Saudi Arabia ranks as one of the world's ten largest military importers in every year for much of the last two decades. New arms agreements are now on the rise with the flood of oil export revenues. [19] Since the Gulf War, Saudi Arabia has dominated the region with respect to deliveries of arms imports relative to those of the other Gulf States; the Kingdom received $7.7 billion in 1999, while the nearest competitor, the United Arab Emirates (UAE), received $950 million in that same year.[20] Just like the other Gulf States, Saudi Arabia has little incentive to try to build major weapons systems themselves, particularly when it can buy some of the most advanced military technology available from American, European, and Russian suppliers.[21] With much of its existing military equipment originating from foreign sources, this dependency on those external sources will most likely continue so long as they not place any effort in arms manufacturing.

Saudi Manpower in Defense

By regional standards, the Saudis possess modern, high-technology forces but do not have the manpower skilled enough to employ them. Saudi regular forces now total some 124,500 men, plus 95,000-100,000 actives in the National Guard and another estimated 130,000 men in the various paramilitary forces. While the Kingdom can fill

---

[19] Anthony H. Cordesman, *The Military Balance in the Middle East* (Westport, Connecticut: Praeger Publishers, 2004), 318.

[20] U.S. Department of State, Bureau of Verification and Compliance, *World Military Expenditures and Arms Transfers 1999-2000*, under "Country Rankings: 1999," http://www.fas.org/man/docs/wmeat9900/index.html (accessed January 31, 2008).

[21] Cordesman and Al-Rodhan, 176.

the military rolls with 6.6 million men that are fit for military service and as 247,000 males a year reach the age of 18, the military forces have serious problems with motivation, education, and training. To man the Saudi forces properly requires a mix of manpower quality and quantity, an approach not fully adopted or routinely followed. They struggle to base modern military training and promotion on performance and merit, rather than birth, family, politics, or social custom.[22] Reversing these manpower trends requires a concerted effort from senior ranking military members that has been relatively non-existent. Thus, Saudi Arabia may have the human resources available to defend its homeland, but may not have the capability to execute effectively without assistance from outside sources.

Overall Assessment for Each Saudi Military Component

Common themes for all the services of the Saudi military arm include deficiencies in training and readiness, as well as a lack of mission focus or understanding of roles, despite its relatively modern and robust size. This section briefly summarizes the capabilities of each Saudi military, and is not intended to capture the nuances that may be highlighted in detailed assessments.

The Saudi Army, or Royal Saudi Land Forces (RSLF), pales in comparison to land forces such as the U.S., British, and Israeli armies, but when compared to a not-so-demanding regional standard, they fare well, not only to nations within the region but many NATO countries that have not seen military action in more than half a century. In general, the RSLF is readjusting its formations to address those threats that arose with the fall of Iraq and those asymmetric ones like infiltrators and terrorists. The RSLF is also

---

[22] Cordesman and Al-Rodhan, 181.

beginning its focus on readiness, training, and sustainability for maneuver warfare, night combat operations, combined arms, and joint warfare. [23]

The Saudi Arabia National Guard (SANG) has similar challenges. Charged with the missions of: maintaining security and stability within the kingdom; defending vital facilities; providing security and a screening force for the kingdom's borders; providing a combat ready internal security force for operations throughout the kingdom; and providing security for the royal family;[24] the SANG is also modifying its attention towards counterterrorism, counterinsurgency and urban warfare. With the rise of a terrorist threat within Saudi Arabia, the SANG is beginning a shirt towards force transformation similar to the U.S.[25]

Although armed with modern, expensive ships and equipment, the Saudi Navy or Royal Saudi Naval Forces (RSNF), was accustomed to being overshadowed in the Gulf by the U.S. and British navies, also finds itself redefining its roles and missions. RSNF is reemphasizing on training and readiness, especially if it is to fulfill the roles as an independent force and the core of a potential naval GCC force. With the main focus of RSNF being defense of the Red Sea, its naval responsibilities will include: protection of critical facilities; mine warfare; ship protection and escort; joint land/air operations; a maritime role in air and missile defense; and anti-amphibious raid operations.[26]

The Saudi Air Force or Royal Saudi Air Force (RSAF), as one of the most technically advanced air force in the Middle East, is still overcoming mishandled overall

---

[23] Cordesman and Al-Rodhan, 193.

[24] Cordesman, *The Military Balance in the Middle East,* 332.

[25] Cordesman and Al-Rodhan, 198.

[26] Cordesman and Al-Rodhan, 205-206.

training and readiness from poor leadership between 1994 and 2001.[27] RSAF's major defects include: an overemphasis on air defense at the expense of offensive air; a failure to operate in the joint environment; a failure to integrate air defense and warfighting capability with other Gulf state; and a failure to rapidly modernize C4I/SR. A reduced air threat environment resulting from Iraq's 2003 defeat and Iran's slow modernization may allow RSAF to consolidate around its most advanced aircraft, creating a smaller and more effective force.[28]

The Saudi Land-Based Air Defenses or Royal Saudi Air Defense Forces (RSADF), operating about 33 surface-to-air missile batteries, has similar problems with joint interoperability like its sister services. With the departure of active U.S. army and air forces from the Kingdom, developing effective air defense capabilities to use its C4 (command, control, communications, and computers) and IS&R (intelligence, surveillance and reconnaissance) assets effectively becomes critical.[29] "The end of the Iraqi threat greatly eases the potential burden on both the Saudi air force and army, however; and Saudi I-Hawk and Patriot units have improved Saudi Arabia's low- to high-level air defense capability along the Gulf coast, while providing some defense against medium-range and theater ballistic missiles.[30] In general, the Kingdom possesses a growing and relatively unseasoned Saudi military that requires much development.

---

[27] Cordesman and Al-Rodhan, 216.

[28] Cordesman and Kleiber, 338-339.

[29] Cordesman and Al-Rodhan, 220.

[30] Cordesman and Kleiber, 338-339.

Chapter Three

3. AN OVERVIEW OF THE ISLAMIC REPUBLIC OF IRAN

It is equally critical to examine particular aspects of Iran to discern the rationale taken by the Saudi leadership with regards to their foreign policy with Iran. In general, the Islamic Republic of Iran, a large and populated country rich in natural resources, remains somewhat militarily hindered, having to recover from a draining eight-year conflict with Iraq, and pursues a less conventional approach to its military apparatus, highlighted by a quest for a ballistic missile capability, as well as a concentration on an irregular warfare capability. The strategic missile and irregular warfare dimensions of Iran's military apparatus are definite assets that separate this nation from all others in the region.

The Islamic Republic of Iran—ITS IMPORTANCE

Iranian Geographical and Resource Significance

With over 68.7 million people,[1] the most obvious characteristic that defines Iran is its Persian, not Arab, character. Dominating both inside and outside the Strait of Hormuz, Iran practically owns the northern Gulf. Its lands serve as a gateway to the rest of Persia, as it shares the borders with Afghanistan, Armenia, Azerbaijan-proper, Azerbaijan-Naxcivan enclave, Iraq, Pakistan, Turkey and Turkmenistan. Iran's abundant energy resources make it a major player in the global energy market, with Iran estimating to hold 11.1% of the world oil reserves (132.0 billion barrels of oil) and 15.3% of the

---

[1] Cordesman and Al-Rodhan, 317.

world's natural gas reserves (970.8 trillion cubic feet).[2] It does not possess the Kingdom's spare petroleum capacity capability.

Iranian Cultural Significance

Iran's history stretches some 2,500 years, with its Persian regal beginnings. Additionally, the other dimension of Iran reflects its Islamic heritage. Both faces of the Iranian Janus reflect Iran at a zenith in self-awareness and world power. For Iran, there is an ever-present goal to recapture its grandeur and providence, believed to have been unfairly taken away with the rise of the West born in the shadow of Persia's eclipse and demise[3] (and this aspect will be revisited in greater detail in later chapters). Driven by Shiite Islamist fundamentalism rather than a Sunni neo-Salafi fundamentalism (present in Saudi Arabia) and a sense of nationalism that is attempting to grasp control over the Gulf, Iran is the region's leading Shiite state at a time of growing sectarian tension.[4] Despite the common acceptance of Islam with Arab nations, this Persian state represents an enduring people that has withstood countless struggles, a distinction Saudi Arabia can not itself claim.

Iranian Political Structure

Unlike the Kingdom of Saudi Arabia, which is monarchical rule, Iran's Republic is guided by a Constitution which identifies a Supreme Leader, who is Commander-in-Chief responsible for general policies and who is elected by the Assembly of Experts. He

---

[2] British Petroleum (BP), *Statistical Review of World Energy,* June 2005, http://www.bp.com/liveassets/bp_internet/switzerland/corporate_switzerland/STAGING/local_assets/down loads_pdfs/s/statistical_review_of_world_energy_2005.pdf (accessed January 31, 2008).

[3] Isaiah Wilson III, "Rediscovering Containment: The Sources of American-Iranian Conduct," *Journal of International Affairs* 60, no. 2 (Spring/Summer 2007): 100-101.

[4] Cordesman and Al-Rodhan, 317-318.

controls intelligence and security operations, has sole power to declare war, appoints and dismisses the heads of judiciary, state radio and television, and appoints half of the Council of Guardians. Iran has a governing infrastructure that resembles a Western democracy, with a President elected by absolute majority in popular ballot, but is second only to the Supreme Leader and leads the executive. Iran also has an elected legislative body in the form of its Parliament and a judicial body in the form of the Council of Guardians. Besides the Supreme Leader position, what is unique about Iran's government is the Assembly of Experts, which is composed of virtuous and learned clerics elected by the public and exists to select the Supreme Leader, and the Expediency Council, which settles disputes between the Parliament and Council of Guardians and advises the Supreme Leader.[5]

The Islamic Republic of Iran—ITS MILITARY CAPABILITY

Iran's conventional military forces represent a conscious decision by the Government of Iran to redirect its focus since its war with Iraq ended in 1988. While Iran's military has quantity by Gulf standards, it lacks quality. Iran's conventional military readiness, effectiveness, and capabilities have declined since the Iran-Iraq War. Iran's efforts to restore its conventional edge continues to fall short relative to its neighbors, as its arms agreements and deliveries declined to $700 million from 1999 to 2002,[6] compared to $4.1 billion for Saudi Arabia during that same period.[7]

---

[5] Dan Smith, *The State of the Middle East* (Los Angeles, California: University of California Press, 2006), 83.

[6] Anthony H. Cordesman and Martin Kleiber, *Iran's Military Forces and Warfighting Capabilities* (Westport, Connecticut: Praeger Security International, 2007), 252.

[7] Cordesman and Kleiber, 318.

A defining moment in Iran's military capability occurred with the Revolution in 1979. The Western powers, included significantly in this group is the United States, stopped all sale of weapons, parts, and munitions to Iran almost immediately, forcing Iran to turn to China, Russia, and other Eastern bloc nations for supplies. The 1980-1988 Iran-Iraq War resulted in the loss of 50 to 60 percent of Iran's land order of battle.[8] Despite major increases in oil revenues, Iran has not militarily reconstituted itself, at least in terms of arms imports. While the creation of its own military industries have had similar impact on its military capabilities, its unimpressive efforts to offset the steady aging of most of its military, compounded by its inability to obtain parts and upgrades for its Western supplied equipment and its lack of parity with the level of weapons and technology of the West and other Gulf forces,[9] have made the nation conventionally vulnerable.

Iranian Manpower in Defense

Although amassing roughly 545,000 military servicemen in 2006, Iran's military manpower problems do exist. Eighteen month conscripts, who offer limited effectiveness because of their limited training, comprise of 220,000 of these forces. A reserve army does not serve this country well since Iran's reserve forces lack the equipment, supplies and leadership cadres to organize and train its reservists. Most of the battle-hardened military personnel of the 1980s have left the service. Also, the current political environment in Iran's government, with deep divisions between moderates and hard-

---

[8] Anthony H. Cordesman, *Iran's Developing Military Capabilities* (Washington, D.C.: Center for Strategic and International Studies, 2005), 1.

[9] Cordesman and Al-Rodhan, 322.

liners, has politicized the armed forces, with overall command of the military remaining under the supreme religious leader, Ayatollah Rouhollah Khomeini.[10] Nevertheless, as the figure below suggests, the Islamic Republic significantly outnumbers the Kingdom as well as all the other Gulf states:

Photo Removed Due to Copyright Restrictions

Figure 3.1: Total Gulf Military Manpower by Country by Service in 2007[11]

Iranian Military Composition

Just like Saudi Arabia, Iran's military apparatus is diverse. Its Iranian Army servicemen are mostly conscripts. The Pasdaran, the Islamic Revolutionary Guards Corps (IRGC) of about 125,000 men, with substantial asymmetric warfare and covert operations capabilities, is the foundation of Iran's hard-line security forces. The IRGC has both military and political units, with close ties to the foreign operations branch of the Iranian Ministry of Intelligence and Security (MOIS), and even plays a major role in Iran's military industries.[12] An Iranian Air Force of 52,000 men operates a numerically strong but aging fleet of about 300 aircraft, and provides limited air force capability (mostly being air-defense and attack missions), coupled with a moderate airlift capability,

---

[10] Cordesman and Al-Rodhan, 322.

[11] Cordesman and Kleiber, 318.

[12] Cordesman, *Iran's Developing Military Capabilities,* 45-47.

the Air Force also operates Iran's land-based air defenses.[13] The even smaller Iranian Navy, with 18,000 provides mine warfare, amphibious warfare, anti-ship missiles, and unconventional warfare as the alternative to compensate for its lack of size, accomplishing the missions aboard 3 frigates, 2 corvettes, 11 missile patrol craft, 5 marine warfare ships, and numerous smaller patrol craft, miniature submarines and amphibious ships [14]

Overall Assessment for Each Iranian Military Component

As described above, the IRGC is the highlight of Iran's military apparatus. Iran's remaining military might lags behind considerably. The Iranian Army has made advancements in its organization, doctrine, training and equipment but it is still hamstrung by a limited armored maneuver capability, artillery forces suited for the static defense and for the use of mass fire, limited sustainment capability, and a mediocre manpower pool. While somewhat capable of power projection, the Iranian Army units are not equipped to be truly expeditionary, as they are riddled by logistics, maintenance, and support systems that must be locally based to operate.[15]

The Iranian Air Force has problems in terms of its sustainability, command and control, and training. Its aging pilot force, operating a fleet that is undergoing unimpressive modernization, lacks advanced training facilities and has only limited capability to conduct realistic training for beyond-visual-range combat and standoff attacks with air-to-surface munitions. The Air Force's land-based air defense, consisting

---

[13] Cordesman and Al-Rodhan, 340.

[14] Cordesman and Kleiber, 108-111.

[15] Cordesman and Al-Rodhan, 335-336.

of Hawks, HQ-21s, SA-5s, Rapiers and Tigers, has quantity, but lacks quality. All of its major systems are based on technology that is now more than 35 years old, vulnerable to U.S. active and passive countermeasures. The Air Force's air defense attempts to overcome some of this vulnerability through improving its C4I systems, jamming, tactics, and radars. [16]

The Iranian Navy, while small, has steadily improved its capability to threaten Gulf shipping and offshore oil facilities. The Navy has sufficient capability to support unconventional warfare and defend its offshore facilities, and islands, and coast line. Although it is still not an effective blue-water navy, it does not need to be in order to threaten or intimidate its neighbors. [17]

The IRGC is Iran's most effective force, which has a land, naval, air, special operations, and civil component. With control over most of Iran's surface-to-surface missiles, the IRGC is believed most importantly to have custody over potentially deployed nuclear weapons, and most or all other chemical, biological, radiological, and nuclear (CBRN) weapons, [18] a contentious issue that draws much debate internationally.

The inadequacies of much of Iran's regular forces compel examination of other military dimensions. Iran's most threatening aspect of its military rests in its weapons of mass destruction (WMD) program. While no "smoking gun" exists that conclusively proves their existence, Iran continues to seek to acquire or develop a means which could deliver them, through long-range ballistic missiles and cruise missiles. [19] For example,

---

[16] Cordesman and Kleiber, 84.

[17] Cordesman and Al-Rodhan, 360.

[18] Cordesman and Kleiber, 73.

[19] Cordesman and Al-Rodhan, 360.

the Iranians created the Shahab-3, designed from the North Korean No Dong medium-range ballistic missile (MRBM) but with a greater payload capacity and range. The Shahab-3 underwent testing by the Islamic Republic in 1997.[20] Additionally, the U.S. government announced its belief that Iran had underground missile factories and was using North Korean, Chinese, and Russian technology, estimating that the progression of Iran's missile program will develop ranges that would make it a global nuclear power, instead of merely a regional power.[21]

---

[20] Charles P. Vick, "Weapons of Mass Destruction- Shahab-3, 3A/Zelzal-3," *GlobalSecurity.org,* February 15, 2007, http://www.globalsecurity.org/wmd/world/iran/shahab-3.htm (accessed March 5, 2008).

[21] "U.S. Consultancy Claims Iran Has Built Underground Missile Factories," *Jane's Missiles and Rockets* (December 8, 2005).

Chapter Four

4. SAUDI ARABIA AND IRAN RELATIONS—A CONTINUOUS EVOLUTION

A snapshot of Saudi Arabia's relations with Iran since the fall of the Shah of Iran in 1979 until the present reveals an interaction driven by self-serving interests. The monarchy in the Kingdom was well intact and with the royal family, there was a definite U.S. ally; the Supreme Leader of the Islamic Republic represented a fresh new look for Iran, one devoid of American influence. After the fall of the Shah, any unions between the Kingdom and the Islamic Republic were to be formed largely for self-protection from an apparent threat such as Iraq. Once the regional environment gets redefined and the threat is no longer valid, any sort of alliance between Iran and Saudi Arabia becomes no longer necessary. This became evident in their behaviors. The Kingdom's pragmatic approach to regional politics has satisfied Saudi Arabia's desire to maintain regional balance.

Islamic Revolution on the Rise

Saudi Arabia was part of a traditional three-way rivalry that existed between itself, Iran and Iraq. Set aside temporarily because of the Iran-Iraq War, the Saudi-Iranian segment of this rivalry revealed itself in not so obvious forms. Relations between these two powerful Middle East countries seemed suspect. Iran's involvement in the Gulf dates back many centuries, and despite foreign efforts to repress the Middle Eastern states from countries such as Great Britain, Iran has sought and continues to seek a restoration of its importance in the Gulf. The second monarch of the Pahlavi dynasty and the last Shah of Iran, Mohammad Reza Pahlavi had ruled since 1941 and during this time was prized by the House of Saud as a buffer against the Soviets and the spread of communism. As a secular rather than religious ruler, the shah had not threatened the Wahhabis of Saudi Arabia with Iran's traditionally competitive Shiite branch of Islam because of the Wahhabis' strong anti-Communist views.[1] Iran and Saudi Arabia recognized Communism as the greater evil they must both overcome first.

With the ouster of Shah Mohammad Reza Pahlavi from Iran in 1979 and the Shah's regime being replaced by the stridently anti-American Islamic regime of Ayatollah Rouhollah Khomeini, this new republic no longer championed Western interests.[2] Iran, as an imperial power, championed Western interests, but as a republic, sought to establish an Islamic order in its own Shiite image. The Islamic dimension of this image would fundamentally appeal to Wahhabi-supported Saudi royalty but because of its Shiite focus, the Iranian aspiration came into direct conflict with Saudi ambitions to dominate the region.[3] Iran threatened Saudi Arabia with its own form of fundamentalism.

Saudi Arabia felt the reach of Ayatollah Khomeini's influence quickly as he began to revolutionize the Shiite minority in the Saudi province of Hasa just across the Persian Gulf from Iran. In the annual pilgrimage to Mecca in 1979, a historic six-week uprising by armed Shiite radicals at the Grand Mosque created the opportunity for the Ayatollah to capitalize on the Shiite population in Hasa. Through program broadcasts from a new fundamentalist radio station—the Voice of Free Iran—Khomeini, the

---

[1] Gerald Posner, *Secrets of the Kingdom* (New York: Random House, 2005), 92.

[2] M.E. Ahrari, *The Gulf and International Security: The 1980s and Beyond* (New York: St Martin's Press, 1989), 1.

[3] M.E. Ahrari, 3.

Supreme Leader, incited the Saudi Shiites into action.[4] The goal was to create an

insurgency against the Saudi authorities who were as treacherous as the Shah was on his

people in Iran.[5] The House of Saud sent in military forces rounded up key agitators in

Mecca and Hasa, and they were publicly beheaded—a clear warning to potential Saudi

political dissidents that rebellion would not be tolerated.[6] While Iran's attempt to incite

revolution in the Kingdom was short lived, further efforts were ceased as growing

concerns on another front—Iran's neighbor, Afghanistan—compelled Iran to keep their

watchful eyes as the Soviets invaded its neighbor in December 1979.[7]

The Kingdom's Initial Response to Iran's Islamic Revolution

While these past events did not jeopardize the Saudi royal family, it still increased

their sense of vulnerability, causing them to have to appease the concerns of their own

fundamentalists. The Kingdom did so by making its policies more conservative. Rules

that became relaxed over the years became more strictly interpreted. Women were

prohibited from appearing on television. All stores and malls had to close completely

during the five daily prayers.[8] The Kingdom distanced itself from the practices of the

West on the domestic front to help regain the confidence of its fundamentalist supporters.

---

[4] Posner, 95-96.

[5] Anthony Cave Brown, *Oil, God, and Gold: The Story of Aramco and the Saudi Kings,* (Boston: Houghton Mifflin, 1999), 344.

[6] Brown, 348-349.

[7] Posner, 97.

[8] Sulaiman Al-Hattlan, "In Saudi Arabia, an Extreme Problem," *Washington Post*, May 8, 2002, 12.

Outside the Kingdom, Saudi Arabia refocused on the matter of their sacred duty to export Wahhabism. A royal directive during this time stated that there were to be "no limits . . . put on expenditures for the propagation of Islam,"[9] and oil revenue was set aside in a grand plan to build Islamic centers, mosques, and schools around the world.[10] What separated the Wahhabi fundamentalist movement abroad from the Islamic revolution of Iran was the message that Saudi Arabia was pursuing a general Islamic revival, initially downplaying the conservative views of Wahhabism. Thus, the Kingdom's message appeared inclusive, rather than exclusive and its base of external supports grew substantially.

Wahhabi fundamentalism became expeditionary. When crisis struck with the Soviet invasion of Afghanistan, Saudi Arabia became the launching point for thousands of fundamentalist volunteers who were making a holy pilgrimage to Afghanistan to fight the foreign infidel army. The Saudis saw the potential for a Wahhabi-based government in Afghanistan. The Saudi government provided enormous sums of money and used its influence with Pakistan's InterServices Intelligence, a U.S. Central Intelligence Agency (CIA) equivalent, in hopes of creating a strong buffer against their Iranian adversary. However, after ten years of fierce battle, victory over the Soviets established a purist Islamic government headed by the Taliban eventually backed by the extremist organization of al-Qaeda, rivaling the rigidness of the most conservative Wahhabis.[11] So not only did the once-supported Taliban threaten its Arab supporters, but it was also

---

[9] David B. Ottaway, "U.S. Eyes Money Trails of Saudi-Backed Charities," *Washington Post*, August 19, 2004, A1.

[10] Posner, 97.

[11] Posner, 98.

viewed as a definite enemy of Iran. Saudi Arabia lost its chance to gain an ally in Afghanistan and helped Iran gain an enemy.

Another opportunity to spread Saudi influence presented itself with the Iraqi invasion of Iran in 1980. While Iraq's Saddam Hussein obsessed with an imperial Iraq that stretched along the borders of the old Ottoman Empire, the Saudis and the Kuwaitis made the invasion of Iran their proxy war, backing Iraq during its agonizing eight years of fighting. Although Iraq was seen as the protector of the Arab nation, the bloody stalemate cost Saudis over $38 billion.[12] Investment in Iraq would cost Saudi Arabia even more because as the attacks spread to Iraq and Iran's oil production facilities, the West compelled the Kingdom to double its oil production in order to drive spiked prices back down from record highs.[13] This reinforced the notion that Saudi Arabia was indeed tied to the West, a notion the House of Saud felt needed to be minimized if it were to be respected by other Arab states.

Iran and Saudi Arabia – On the Same Side

While during the 1980s both Saudi Arabia and Iraq fought the Islamic Republic of Iran and its efforts to export its radical version of Islam, the 1990s would bring Iran and Saudi Arabia back together again in order to prevent domination by Iraq's Saddam Hussein. When Iran accepted terms of an immediate ceasefire postulated by UN Security Council Resolution 598 in July 1988, the Iranian leadership found themselves in a desperate military and economic situation, requiring a refocus of national priorities. With the eventual election of Hojjat al-Islam Rafsanjani as President of the Republic, Iran

---

[12] Said K. Aburish, *The Rise, Corruption and Coming Fall of the House of Saud* (New York: St. Martin's/Griffin, 2003), 139.

[13] Posner, 99.

shifted its energy to the reconstruction of the country, which required stimulating the international community to be economically active with Iran.[14] Rafsanjani showed no real interest in the pursuit of Khomeini's messianic goals and he appeared to want to limit his attachment to these goals to the rhetorical level.[15] The religious factors which had played so vital a role in Iran's foreign policy caught little attention. The purely national interests of Iran embodied in the new "Era of Reconstruction," for which cooperation with potential regional and international partners was necessary, overcame the radical philosophy of the revolution.[16] "Rafsanjani and his supporters now interpreted export of the revolution primarily as an obligation to strengthen the revolution in Iran according to the new creed: if the Islamic Republic became attractive to other Muslims, the revolution would spread by merely setting a successful example."[17]

Within days after the ceasefire of the Iran-Iraq War, there was a general Iranian desire to improve the crumbling relations between the neighboring states. As Iran struggled to revitalize its friendships with Arab states like Kuwait and Saudi Arabia, the very nation that was Iran's scorn—Iraq—would threaten one of its most recent allies with the invasion of Kuwait in August of 1990.[18] Fearful of Saddam's true intentions, the Kingdom gracefully accepted the reestablishment of open dialogue with Iran. The Arab nations and members of the international community spent their resources on expelling

---

[14] Henner Fürtig, *Iran's Rivalry with Saudi Arabia Between the Gulf Wars* (United Kingdom: Garnet Publishing Limited, 2002), 94.

[15] R.W. Cottam, "Charting Iran's New Course," *Current History,* 90, no. 1 (1991), 37.

[16] Fürtig, 94.

[17] Fürtig, 95.

[18] Fürtig, 96.

Saddam's forces out of Kuwait. Meanwhile, Iran enjoyed being the recipient of an

aggressive Iraq having to buy the tolerance of a neighbor. Iraq had to concede many

unsettled disputes between itself and Iran, such as withdrawal of all forces to

internationally recognized borders. Although not directly involved in this Gulf crisis,

Iran continued to benefit from it:

> The Iraqi invasion of Kuwait and the radically altered balance of power in the
> Gulf region after the Second Gulf War acted as catalysts improving exchanges
> between Iran and Saudi Arabia. Iraq now proved to be an even greater threat to
> Saudi Arabia than it had been during the 1970s. Iran's leadership followed the
> dictum that the enemy of my enemy is my friend and the détente with Saudi
> Arabia thus became one of its most remarkable successes during the Kuwait
> crisis, with full diplomatic relations between both countries restored on 19 March
> 1991.[19]

Iran's leadership fully embraced this need for stability along the borders and good

relations with its neighbors. In December 1997, the newly elected Mohammad Khatami

continued his predecessor's policy of careful fence building with an Islamic summit in

Tehran, where Saudi Arabian Crown Prince Abdullah's attendance would eventually

foster into a bilateral agreement between the two countries. This agreement emphasized

cooperation in security matters, including the control of terrorism, money laundering,

smuggling and drug trafficking.[20] Additionally, Iran relaxed its efforts to encourage

Saudi Shiite unrest and terrorism, halted its attacks on the Saudi royal family, and

stopped supporting riots and protests during the Hajj.[21]

---

[19] Fürtig, 102-103.

[20] Robert O. Freedman, *The Middle East Enters the Twenty-First Century* (Gainesville, Florida: University Press of Florida, 2002), 56-57.

[21] Anthony H. Cordesman, *Saudi Arabia Enters the Twenty-First Century* (Connecticut: Praeger Publishers, 2003), 45.

At the turn of the century, Iran's efforts to break out of a growing isolation were well received by the Kingdom, particularly in the area of oil policy. In early 2000, Saudi demands for adjustments to oil production quotas within OPEC brought about disagreement, but never to the extent of an OPEC split. Saudi Arabia maintained a rapprochement with Iran with the full understanding that any forceful Saudi behavior may provoke Iran to lead efforts to intimidate Saudi Arabia or its neighbors or even to attempt to win influence with Saudi Arabia's Shiites, just as it did in the 1980s.[22]

Saudi Arabia's Renewed Concerns

Although securing the Iran-Iraq border progressed and OPEC relations appeared somewhat accommodating, the growing perspective from Tehran at the turn of the century was that serious regional threats still remain. Haunted by the perennial fear of an encirclement by hostile powers, Iran speculated the effects of the regional situation that included a menacing Iraq; an unstable Afghanistan and Pakistan; the emerging nuclear capabilities of India and Pakistan; the acquiring of large quantities of advanced weaponry by Saudi Arabia and Kuwait; the U.S. military presence in the Persian Gulf; and Israel's military cooperation with Turkey. Once again, the Iranian leadership recognized the dangers surrounding its country and thus shifted its focus. Specifically, Khomeini's successor as Supreme Leader, Ayatollah Khamenei, sought to bolster Iran's leadership credentials by championing Islamic movements elsewhere in the world, speaking out on causes important to Muslims, opposing U.S. and Great-Power influence in Muslim states,

---

[22] Cordesman, *Saudi Arabia Enters the Twenty-First Century*, 50.

preventing the plundering of the resources of Muslim countries by outside powers, and resisting the West's so-called cultural onslaught against the Muslim world.[23]

The Supreme Leader's desire to champion Islamic movements has manifested itself into the present-day regional security situation, highlighted by three specific arenas, which compel Saudi Arabia to respond. First, Iraqi Shiites with close religious ties to Tehran are in power in Baghdad, replacing Sunni domination that had lasted for decades. Second, the inconclusive outcome of the 34-day war of 2006 between Israel and Hezbollah, heavily supported by Iran, enabled the Party of God's leadership to claim victory over the mighty Israeli Defense Forces. In the aftermath of the war, Hezbollah's popularity and Iran's popularity have substantially increased among Arab masses. Finally, Harajat al-Muqawama al-Islamiya (HAMAS), which, like Iran, does not recognize Israel, controls the Gaza Strip and challenges the diplomatic approach adopted by Palestinian Authority President Mahmoud Abbas and supported by moderate Sunni Arab states, particularly Egypt, Jordan, and Saudi Arabia.[24]

Iranian President Mahmoud Ahmadinejad has made considerable progress with the Palestinian issue in particular:

> By offering aid and comfort to HAMAS and Hezbollah, and organizing a bizarre conference on "A world without Zionism and America" in October 2005 and an even stranger gathering on "Review of the Holocaust: A Global Vision" in December 2006, he [Ahamadinejad] has tried to enhance Iran's leadership status in the Muslim world. By portraying the Islamic Republic to the masses in Gaza and the Occupied Territory as a Shiite and non-Arab government spearheading

---

[23] Freedman, 57-58.

[24] Gawdat Bahgat, "Saudi Arabia and the Arab-Israeli Peace Process," *Middle East Policy* XIV, no. 3 (2007): 49.

the cause of Sunni Arabs, he has attempted to eclipse Egypt, Jordan and Saudi Arabia—three Sunni states—which fie for the title of Palestine's "savior."[25]

---

[25] Jahangir Amuzegar, "The Ahmadinejad Era: Preparing for the Apocalypse," *Journal of International Affairs* 60, no.2 (Spring/Summer 2007): 48.

Chapter Five

5. SAUDI ARABIA'S CURRENT FOREIGN POLICY APPROACH WITH IRAN

Saudi Arabia's House of Saud has been and will continue to impact the leadership of the Islamic Republic of Iran. The Kingdom's leadership understands the importance of countering the messages of Iran. While the Kingdom's military might is gradually on the rise, Saudi Arabia's position within the region as a military player, particularly as a single state actor, is unproven. Saudi Arabia must employ other means of national power.

The Kingdom seeks to offset Iranian influence through indirect and direct means. Powered by wealth from Saudi oil and recognition as the informal lead voice of the Arab world, King Abdullah has the ability to catch the attention of the impressionable. In unstable areas within the region, where there are target audiences that wish their goals to be acknowledged and validated such as in the Gaza Strip, King Abdullah advocates peaceful negotiation versus violent rebellion advocated by Iran. However, in a more sectarian environment such as Iraq, his support for the Sunni Iraqis is much more emphatic, driven by a strong sense of loyalty to the Sunni community.

When the Kingdom is at a marked disadvantage, such as in its military capabilities, its common ethnic bond with the nations of the Arabian Peninsula becomes a resource from which to strengthen its soft power. Saudi Arabia utilizes exclusive Arab organizations like the GCC to advance its agenda. And when it comes to direct lines of communication between the leaders of both the Kingdom and the Islamic Republic, Saudi Arabia ensures that this avenue is open and this is evident in the Saudi-Iran interactions noted in this chapter. The scope of this research cites the Kingdom's indirect and direct diplomatic, military and economic efforts to keep Iran's influence in check.

Indirect Diplomatic Efforts

While much of the international community pays attention to the nuclear ambitions and missile programs of Iran, the Islamic Republic's soft power causes great concern to the neighboring Arab states. Although it may be hard to assess Tehran's Shiite breadth of influence, the Sunni Gulf leaders do worry. The King of the Hashemite Kingdom of Jordan, King Abdullah II bin Al Hussein, warns against the rise of a "Shiite Crescent." Likewise, the President of the Arab Republic of Egypt, President Hosni Mubarak, questions the loyalty of the Arab Shiites in its own government. Saudi Arabia recognizes Shiite presence in its lands as something that can not be neglected, and it knows the importance of maintaining a grip on its own Shiite community. King Abdullah of Saudi Arabia has taken many initiatives to improve the socioeconomic and political conditions of the Saudi Shiite community, to include allowing the building of Shiite mosques and permitting the public celebration of Shiite religious festivals such as Ashoura. Despite these types of efforts, regional sectarian strife may undercut any gains from the initiatives.[1] King Abdullah can not ignore Iran's potential influence in his kingdom.

Saudi Arabia, since late 2006, has made itself a key player in the previously mentioned stalemates in Iraq, Lebanon, and Palestine. "Saudi diplomats have participated in negotiations to bring peace to Iraq and reach a compromise between the Lebanese rivals. Saudi efforts to end fighting between Palestinian factions and to broker

---

[1] Bahgat, 55.

a comprehensive Arab-Israeli peace agreement have occupied a central stage in Middle East policy."[2] This section will examine Saudi Arabia's involvement in these crises.

The Arab-Israeli peace process has taken multiple routes without resounding regional success. In 1979, Egyptian President Anwar al-Sadat signed a bilateral peace treaty with Israel, a move largely condemned by most Arab states. Because of concern over rising radicalization and polarization of the Arab world, Saudi leaders offered their own version of a comprehensive peace. The Saudi proposal, first presented by King Fahd in the 1980s and known as the Fahd Peace Plan, was an alternative that would outline a framework for a comprehensive peace between the Arabs and Israel. The Egyptian peace process in 1979 met strong resistance from the Arab masses but this Arab initiative of King Fahd brought about no results.[3] After September 11, 2001 dealt a heavy blow to American-Saudi relations, the redesigned Saudi Peace Initiative (SPI), now known as the Abdullah Plan and named after Fahd's successor, has multiple purposes, now serving not only as a conciliatory gesture toward Israel, but it could also defuse the tension and improve the country's image. Instead of a mere recognition of the Jewish state in the Middle East, as offered by the Fahd Plan, the new plan offered Israel full peace, including political, economic and cultural normalization.[4]

In this situation, the Kingdom has taken a strategic opportunity because of the innate hostility that existed between the Islamic Republic of Iran and the Jewish state, both seeing the other as its sworn enemies. An Arab offer of full peace along with

---

[2] Bahgat, 49.

[3] Bahgat, 51-52.

[4] The Royal Embassy of Saudi Arabia, "The Arab Peace Initiative," *Middle East Policy* IX, no. 2 (June 2007): 25-26.

normalization equates to the abandoning of the Islamic Republic to a certain degree. Iran's rising influence in Iraq, in Lebanon and with HAMAS since the early 2000s has posed both regional and domestic challenges to Saudi Arabia. Pursuit of a comprehensive solution to the Arab-Israeli conflict with Saudi Arabia as the lead promoter will help contain this threat and will likely enhance the Kingdom's standing both in the region and on the international scene. It is important to note that this plan is mainly a declaration of principles, not a detailed proposal.[5] Nevertheless, the proposal sends the signals of an Arab community willing to negotiate a comprehensive peace with Israel, thereby weakening Iran's soft power influences in Lebanon and Palestine.

The Kingdom's relationships with HAMAS and Hezbollah seem fragile because of the Iranian dimension, and King Abdullah has taken a pragmatic approach in dealing with these two groups. For example, after the U.S. and the European Union designated HAMAS as a terrorist organization and HAMAS won the majority in the Palestinian elections, the Saudi government cut off its aid to avoid controversy. This brought HAMAS and Iran closer, as the Islamic Republic provided badly needed aid to the Palestinians.[6] Concerned about the connection between HAMAS and Fatah, King Abdullah brought HAMAS's Prime Minister Haniya and Fatah's President Abbas to a summit in Mecca and brokered a power-sharing pact, where the King also promised one billion dollars in aid to the Palestinians.[7] When the Hezbollah fighters kidnapped two Israel soldiers, leading eventually to a 34-day war with Israel in 2006, Saudi Arabia first

---

[5] Bahgat, 53.

[6] Bahgat, 56.

[7] Helene Cooper, "After the Mecca Accord, Clouded Horizons," *The New York Times*, July 17, 2006.

sharply criticized Hezbollah for initiating the attack in the hopes of preventing further escalation. However, as the civilian death toll climbed and support for Hezbollah grew, that prompted the Saudi stand to change to a condemnation of Israel and a pledging of one and a half billion dollars to support Lebanon's economy and fund rebuilding efforts.[8] A brokered Arab-Israeli peace will ease these types of regional challenges for the Kingdom.

The Saudis do not pursue a pragmatic approach to the situation in Iraq. Following the invasion of Iraq in 2003 and the establishment of a Shiite-dominated government in Baghdad, Saudi leaders have expressed deep concern about the fate of the Iraqi Sunnis, believing that the right approach for containing the prevalent sectarian strife is to empower the Iraqi Sunnis. The Saudi leaders viewed Iraqi Prime Minister Nouri al-Maliki as someone too tied to Iran and pro-Iranian Shiite parties to bring about real reconciliation with Iraqi Sunnis. Thus, prominent Islamic clerics from Saudi Arabia called on Sunni Muslims around the Middle East to support their brethren in Iraq against Shiites and praised the insurgency, causing the funding for Sunni insurgency to come from private individuals in Saudi Arabia and the Gulf states. The Saudi leaders even warned the U.S. that an American withdrawal from Iraq will result in massive Saudi intervention to stop Iranian-backed Shiite militias from butchering Iraqi Sunnis.[9]

There is already Sunni persecution in Iraq's western region.[10] Saudi suspicions of Iranian-backed activity in this Sunni dominant al-Anbar Province are not without merit.

---

[8] Faiza Saleh Ambah, "Many Arabs Applaud Hezbollah," *The Washington Post,* May 11, 2007.

[9] Nawaf Obaid, "Stepping Into Iraq," *The Washington Post,* November 29, 2006.

[10] Nir Rosen, "The Flight From Iraq," *The New York Times,* May 13, 2007, http://www.nytimes.com/2007/05/13/magazine/13refugees-t.html?pagewanted=10&r=1&fta=y (accessed February 13, 2008).

The Anbar Awakening, whereby the Iraqi Sunnis have decided to lend its support to the American Coalition against the insurgency efforts, is in direct response to the pro-Iranian threat in their locality. Iranian influence has infiltrated the al-Anbar Province, attempting to consecrate division and civil war, and it is evident even in the media. The Iraqi Satellite, Al-Fada-iyah al-Iraqiyah, is the official state-run television station, currently under the hegemony of pro-Iranian militias, and has made it a place to hurl insults and vent sectarian poison. Analysts have linked the 2007 murders of al-Anbar shaykhs, to include Shaykh Abu-Rishah, to the Iraqi Satellite, who sent photography crews to film Shakh Abu Rishah. Iraqi Satellite involvement with the people of al-Anbar served more to enable intelligence services and militias than to show genuine interest.[11] The unfortunate killings of highly-respected al-Anbar shaykhs have solidified U.S. and Iraqi-Sunni efforts to stabilize their region.

The Kingdom recognizes the importance of countering the influence of Iran and does so through strategic messaging that is embedded in its diplomacy with Middle East nations in crisis. The diplomatic efforts communicate to its target audience, such as HAMAS and Hezbollah, that there are peaceful alternatives to crisis. Rather than sponsoring or advocating continued unrest in unstable regions like Lebanon and Palestine, King Abdullah contests such Iranian sponsorship by attempting to settle disputes. However, Saudi Arabia does not hesitate to aid its external Sunni contemporaries against its Shiite rivals when it is warranted.

---

[11] Khudayr Tahir, "Did the Iraqi Satellite Channel spy on Abu Rishah," *British Broadcasting Corporation Worldwide Monitoring,* September 16, 2007, http://www.lexisnexis.com/us/Inacademic/results/docview/docview.do?risb=21_T3196545951&format=G NBF&sort=RELEVANCE&startDocNo=1&resultsUrlKey=29_T3196545956&cisb=22_T3196545955&tre eMax=true&treeWidth=0&csi=10962&docNo=1 (accessed February 13, 2008).

Indirect Military Efforts

Just like those of other Arabian Peninsula states, Saudi Arabia's developing military apparatus is not quite a respectable deterrent to the Islamic Republic of Iran. However, a combination of military capabilities from multiple states does rapidly increase the overall defense capability for all involved. A union of existing military forces equates to relatively quick implementation of existing state-of-the-art equipment from each nation at a relatively low cost, particularly when compared to fielding new forces from scratch.

The GCC maintains a military force called the Peninsula Shield, founded in 1986 during the Iran-Iraq war. Although consisting of only 9000 troops usually based in Saudi Arabia, this force consists of military members from all the GCC countries and it did assist in the liberation of Kuwait in the 1991 Gulf War and also redeployed there at the start of Operation Iraqi Freedom (OIF).[12] At the proposal of Saudi King Abdullah in the fall of 2006,[13] the military chiefs of staff of the GCC members agreed to develop Peninsula Shield into a 22,000 service member force. This reorganized Peninsula Shield is meant to have each of the members complement one another within the standing force. It will also feature airlift and naval power, two capabilities it currently lacks.[14] While issues such as interoperability and overall command and control of the Peninsula Shield are under discussion, this expansion offers Saudi Arabia a military option that if exercised, would symbolize Arab approval. A growing combined GCC military force

---

[12] Riad Kahwaji, "GCC Creates Quick-Reaction Force," *Defense News,* February 4, 2008.

[13] M. Ghazanfar Ali Khan, "GCC to Discuss 'Peninsula Shield' Expansion," *Arab News,* November 2, 2006, http://www.arabnews.com/?page=4&section=0&article=83184&d=2&m=11&y=2006 (accessed February 13, 2008).

[14] Kahwaji, "GCC Creates Quick-Reaction Force."

conveys to all potential adversaries such as Iran an increasing commitment to the defense of the Arabian Peninsula.

Direct Diplomatic Efforts

Diplomatically, an open line of communication with the Islamic Republic continues to be the overall theme for the Kingdom. "Tough talk" with directive overtones does not appeal to King Abdullah. Rather, he prefers an open dialogue highlighted by a willingness to listen and express the ideas and concerns of both sides. It is a very patient approach to diplomacy, often demonstrated in the smallest and subtlest of steps. For example, the Kingdom of Saudi Arabia's invitation to Iranian President Ahmadinejad to attend the recent hajj pilgrimage to Mecca demonstrates the independent-minded rule of King Abdullah to pursue diplomatic initiatives in cooperation with Iran. Head-on confrontation is not the way they wish to deal with the Iran problem. [15] King Abdullah's key leaders, such as Foreign Minister Prince Saud al-Faisal currently sets a positive tone, saying that the Kingdom wants to maintain peaceful ties with Iran. Even the most recent tension between Washington and Tehran regenerated in the Strait of Hormuz in January 2008 did little to effect the King's attitude. When warned of Iran's aggressive ambitions from President Bush, Prince Saud emphasized that "Saudi Arabia is a neighbor of Iran in the Gulf, which is a small lake. We are keen that harmony and peace should prevail among states of the region."[16]

---

[15] Borzou Daragahi, "Bush fails to persuade Arab allies," Los Angeles Times, January 19, 2008, http://www.latimes.com/new/printedition/asection/la-fg-iran19jan19,5232944,print.stor (accessed January 31, 2008).

[16] Agence France-Presse, "Bush seen facing difficult talks during Riyadh visit," *Gulf Times,* January 14, 2008, http://www.gulf-times.com/site/topics/article.asp?cu_no=2&item_no=195586&version=1&template_id=37&parent_id=17, (accessed January 31, 2008).

Saudi King speaks to Iranian officials with frankness, reminding them of the fragile region that exists. King Abdullah met with senior Iranian official All Larijani in Riyadh advising him not to expose the region to dangers and advised him that although the Kingdom does not interfere in anyone's affairs, any state which resorts to unwise acts will have to bear the responsibility in front of other countries in the region.[17] With issues of international concern, such as the possible nuclear weapons development of the Islamic Republic, Saudi Arabia maintains a guarded level of trust and understanding with Iran. The Kingdom acknowledges that the necessary purpose of Iran's nuclear efforts is for alternative energy needs but also discusses with Iran the danger of introducing nuclear weapons to the Middle East.[18]

Direct communication, regardless of the issues, culturally demonstrates respect. Interaction between the two nations, at many senior levels, fosters greater understanding of each other's perspective and reduces the likelihood of regional differences to morph into harsh disagreements and aggressive actions.

Indirect Economic Efforts

Nations like Iran that have considerable impact on the petroleum world are likewise susceptible to radical changes in petroleum policy. Economic pressure on Iran, afforded to Saudi Arabia due to its stature in the petroleum industry, provides another avenue to effect the perceived Iranian threat. "In light of regional conflict and high oil

---

[17] Middle East Economic Digest, "Gaining Confidence," *Middle East Economic Digest* 51, no. 7 (February 16, 2007): 41-43, http://ezproxy6.ndu.edu/login?url=http://search.ebscohost.com/login.aspx?direct=true&db=bsh&AN=24360442&site=ehost-live (accessed October 24, 2007).

[18] Islamic Republic News Agency, "Iran-Saudi Arabian parliamentary friendship group hold meeting in Riyadh," January 27, 2008, http://www2.irna.ir/en/news/view/menu-234/0801271690004753.htm (accessed February 15, 2008).

prices, the Saudi leadership has issued a directive to increase oil production so as to mitigate the effects of major potential supply disruptions from four key exporters: Iran, Venezuela, Nigeria and Iraq."[19] The Saudi-US Relations Information Service (SUSRIS), an independent, private-sector information resource, offering comprehensive news and information on the history, breadth and depth of the U.S.-Saudi Arabia relationship released a brief conducted by Nawaf Obaid, the Director of the Saudi National Security Assessment Project, a government consultancy based in Riyadh. In this project, Obaid examined Saudi Arabia's Strategic Energy Initiative, noting that "Before the end of 2007, Saudi Arabia is expected to have enough spare capacity to offset Iranian exports. By 2008-2009, the goal is to satisfy global demand during a potential disruption from Iran and one of the three other major OPEC exporters (Venezuela, Nigeria or Iraq)."[20] By carrying most of the potential burden that may be caused by the four key exporters above, Saudi Arabia sends a signal to Iran and any other nation that wishes to manipulate the petroleum industry that it will not tolerate this kind of economic disruption.

Saudi Arabia's economic influence on Iran manifests itself in other ways. The GCC recently decided to launch a common market, expecting to draw more foreign investment to the region. The six-nation GCC had a combined gross domestic product of over US$553 billion in 2005.[21] The GCC Secretary-General Abdul Rahman Al-Attiyah described the launch of the Gulf Common Market on January 1, 2008 as historic, adding

---

[19] Bahgat, 57.

[20] Nawaf Obaid, *Saudi Arabia's Strategic Energy Initiative: Safeguarding Against Supply Disruptions,* (Riyadh, Saudi Arabia: Saudi National Security Assessment Project, 2006), 2, http://www.saudi-us-relations.org/fact-book/documents/2006/060904-snsap-energy-initiative.pdf (accessed January 31, 2008).

[21] The Associated Press, "Six Arab Gulf states to announce common market in December," *International Herald Tribune,* October 10, 2007, http://www.iht.com/articles/ap/2007/10/10/business/ME-GEN-Gulf-Common-Market.php (accessed January 31, 2008).

that it would ensure "economic equality" among GCC citizens. Decided during a GCC summit in December 2007, this GCC Common Market aims to raise production, efficiency, and optimum usage of available resources, as well as to improve the GCC's negotiating position in international economic forums. The Common Market gives GCC nationals freedom of movement, residency, and employment in all six countries.[22] This is an exclusive measure that further minimizes Iran's ability to wield its influence in these Arab nations, since the Islamic Republic is not a GCC member.

---

[22] P.K. Abdul Ghafour, "GCC Common Market Becomes a Reality," *Arab News,* January 1, 2008, http://www.arabnews.com/?page=1&section=0&article=105173&d=1&m=1&y=2008 (accessed January 31, 2008).

Chapter Six

6. UNITED STATES'S CURRENT FOREIGN POLICY APPROACH WITH IRAN

President George W. Bush refers to the Islamic Republic of Iran in his National

Security Strategy for 2006 as a tyrannical regime. He boldly professed that this:

> Regime sponsors terrorism; threatens Israel; seeks to thwart Middle East peace; disrupts democracy in Iraq; and denies the aspirations of its people for freedom. The nuclear issue and our other concerns can ultimately be resolved only if the Iranian regime makes the strategic decision to change these policies, open up its political system, and afford freedom to its people . . . Our strategy is to block the threats posed by the regime while expanding our engagement and outreach to the people the regime is oppressing.[1]

Confrontational as this strategy is, this summarizes the overall approach the

administration has pursued since the attacks on 11 September 2001.

The Bush administration's policy succeeded a policy that was highlighted by a

Bill Clinton administration which failed to begin any high level talks with Iran. The U.S.

continues to capitalize on opportunities to reestablish ties under Bush as well. From 9/11

there arose a shared enemy for the U.S. and Iran in the form of the militant Sunni Muslim

fundamentalism in Afghanistan. Senior U.S. and Iranian diplomats acknowledged

cooperation in restructuring the Afghan government. Militarily, there was even tacit

collaboration. Rather than continue such positive momentum towards communication,

G.W. Bush reversed this policy trend.[2] Richard Haas, a Bush Department of State

director for policy planning advocated an end to blocking Iran's application to join the

World Trade Organization (WTO)[3] but the Bush administration rejected the idea. Even

---

[1] George W. Bush, *National Security Strategy of the United States of America*, (March 16, 2006): 20-21.

[2] Barbara Slavin, *Bitter Friends, Bosom Enemies—Iran, the U.S. and the Twisted Path to Confrontation* (New York: St. Martin's Press, 2007): 4.

prominent Americans such as President Bush's own father were unable to convince the current administration to consider a diplomatic path. Ideologues that favored a more "Ramboesque" approach took hold of foreign policy, placing Iran in an "Axis of Evil" with North Korea and Iraq.[4] Driven by Iran's behavior as a rogue nation and a nation pursuing a WMD capability, the United States executes policies with and without the support of international partners.

Unilateral Action

The U.S. position as a dominant world figure allows it to exercise unilateral restrictions on Iran.

> Since 1987, U.S. agencies have implemented numerous sanctions . . . First, Treasury oversees a ban on U.S. trade and investment with Iran and filed over 94 civil penalty cases between 2003 and 2007 against companies violating the prohibition . . . Second, State administers laws that sanction foreign parties engaging in proliferation or terrorism-related activities with Iran. Under one law, State has imposed sanctions in 111 instances against Chinese, North Korean, and Russian entities. Third, Treasury or State can use financial sanctions to freeze the assets of targeted parties and reduce their access to the U.S. financial system.[5]

The U.S. strategic message suggested by these sanctions are clear— U.S. companies that choose to not adhere to its strict prohibitive guidance will face civil prosecution and foreign companies that do the same will not be immune and will be isolated as well. It is important to note that although U.S. agencies can disrupt assets, a ban may be

---

[3] Richard N. Haas, "What to Do With American Primacy," *Foreign Affairs,* 78, no.5 (September/October 1999).

[4] Slavin, 4.

[5] U.S. Government Accountability Office, "Iran Sanctions—Impact in Furthering U.S. Objectives Is Unclear and Should Be Reviewed," *Report to the Ranking Member, Subcommittee on National Security and Foreign Affairs, House Committee on Oversight and Government Reform,* December 2007 (Washington, DC: Government Printing Office, 2007): 2, http://www.gao.gov/highlights/d0858high.pdf (accessed February 10, 2008).

circumvented by shipping U.S. goods to Iran through other countries. However, a sanction still makes it difficult for a determined party to overcome.

Iran definitely feels the effects of these American restrictions, despite all the maneuvering to circumvent them. The United States Government Accountability Office (GAO) reported to the Subcommittee on National Security and Foreign Affairs for the House Committee on Oversight and Reform in December 2007, highlighting several specific impacts on Iran because of the sanctions.

> First, U.S. officials report that U.S. sanctions have slowed foreign investment in Iran's petroleum sector, which hinders Iran's ability to fund proliferation and terrorism-related activities. Second, financial sanctions deny parties involved in Iran's proliferation and terrorism activities access to the U.S. financial system and complicate their support for such activities. Third, U.S. officials have identified broad impacts, such as providing a clear statement of U.S. concerns about Iran.[6]

Much of the above reporting are assessments in very general terms. Quantifying the effects in these three areas in particular are difficult to determine.

As optimistic as the aforementioned impacts may suggest to U.S. policy makers, other evidence questions the actual extent of these impacts. A globalized market allows for Iran to pursue non-U.S. options that are equally lucrative.

> Since 2003, the Iranian government has signed contracts reported at approximately $20 billion with foreign firms to develop its energy resources . . . In addition, sanctioned Iranian banks may be able to turn to other financial sources or fund their activities in currencies other that the U.S. dollar. U.S. and international reports also find that Iran continues proliferation activities and support for terrorism.[7]

Additionally, while broad assessments on sanctions suggest an effect approach, only the Department of the Treasury actually conducts assessments of its sanctions in the financial

---

[6] U.S. Government Accountability Office, 18.

[7] U.S. Government Accountability Office, 18.

arena, under the directives of Executive Orders 13382 and 13224. Other U.S. agencies

do not assess the impact of sanctions in helping achieve U.S. objectives nor collect data

demonstrating the direct results of their sanctioning and enforcement actions.[8]

GAO suggests that U.S. sanctions to pressure Iran, therefore, are insufficient:

"Iran's global trade ties and leading role in energy production make it difficult for
the United States to isolate Iran and deter its acquisition of advanced weapons
technology and support for terrorism. First, Iran's trade with the world—both
imports and exports—has grown since the U.S. trade ban began in 1987.
Although trade has fluctuated from year to year, most of the growth has occurred
since 2002, coinciding with the rise in oil prices. This trade includes imports or
weapons and nuclear technology. Second, global interest in purchasing and
developing Iran's substantial petroleum reserves has kept Iran active in global
commerce."[9]

Multilateral efforts targeting Iran complements a gradually deteriorating, unilateral U.S.

approach.

Multilateral Action

While the "Axis of Evil" rhetoric has toned down considerably, the U.S. imposes

diplomatic and economic pressure on the Islamic Republic of Iran in the international

stage, particularly with respect to Iran's pursuit of weapons of mass destruction (WMD).

Bush's policy promotes multilateral action against proliferation, which is not limited in

scope to Iran. Anti-proliferation efforts sponsored or driven by the U.S. are on numerous

fronts. The U.S. provides financial assistance to states to eliminate weapons and prevent

their spread through the Department of Energy's (DOE) nuclear material security work.

---

[8] U.S. Government Accountability Office, 18.

[9] U.S. Government Accountability Office, 26.

[10] Under the formation in 2002 of the G8 Global Partnership Against the Spread of Weapons and Materials of Mass Destruction, an initiative agreed upon by Canada, France, Germany, Italy, Japan, Russia, United Kingdom, the U.S. and the European Union (EU), the G8 addresses non-proliferation, disarmament, counter-terrorism, and nuclear safety issues.[11]

The largest and most significant multilateral instrument employed by the U.S. resides in the United Nations and its Security Council, as the U.S. has sponsored many of the U.N. anti-proliferation initiatives. The U.S. spearheaded the effort within the United Nations Security Council with Resolution 1540, which requires all states to criminalize WMD proliferation, institute effective export controls, and enhance security for nuclear materials.[12] UNSC Resolutions 1737 and 1747 succeeded 1540 as Iran's quest for a nuclear capability continued. The U.S. strengthened the International Atomic Energy Agency's (IAEA) ability to detect, and respond to, nuclear proliferation by instituting the effort to increase the IAEA's safeguard budget, and by calling for universal adoption of the Additional Protocol and the creation of a new special committee of the IAEA Board to examine ways to strengthen the Agency's safeguards and verification capabilities. The U.S. also helped to restore the essential role of the U.N. Security Council in addressing noncompliance with IAEA safeguards and nuclear Nonproliferation Treaty (NPT)

---

[10] Robert G. Joseph, Office of the Under Secretary for Arms Control and International Security, "The Bush Administration Approach to Combating the Proliferation of Weapons of Mass Destruction, (remarks, Carnegie International Nonproliferation Conference, Washington, DC, November 7, 2005), under "Effective Multilateral Action Against Proliferation," http://www.state.gov/t/us/rm/56584.htm (accessed February 10, 2008).

[11] G8, Kananaskis Summit -2002, "The G8 global partnership against the spread of weapons and materials of mass destruction," 2002, http://www.g8.fr/evian/english/navigation/g8_documents/archives_from_...against_the_spread_of_weapns _and _materials_of_mass_destruction.html (accessed February 12, 2008).

[12] Joseph, 2.

obligations.[13] Through broad diplomatic efforts such as these, the U.S. receives general support from a vocal majority in the international community for Bush's approach to combating WMD proliferation. It is important to note, however, that this general support is not always automatic or guaranteed. Much time is spent on debating the mandates within the UNSC Resolutions.

Whether done multilaterally or unilaterally, the prevailing theme of the multilateral measures remained largely repressive and there seems to be no need to abandon this methodology when it has been successful in the past. Exclusion through sanctions coupled with disengagement at the senior leadership levels proved to be an effective method for another threat—Libya. Seen as a state that sponsored terrorism and possessed a WMD program, Libya took substantial steps in 2004 to eliminate its WMD programs and longer range missiles and halt all support for terrorism. As a result, President Bush terminated the applications of the Iran and Libya Sanctions Act with respect to Libya, and the Treasury Department modified sanctions imposed on U.S. firms and individuals to allow the resumption of most commercial activities, financial transactions, and investments. Besides enhancing economic relations, the U.S. began to initiate a dialogue on trade, investment, and economic reform, as well as encourage the global market to reintegrate Libya through ceasing to object its efforts to begin the WTO accession process.[14] Only after submission to U.S. demands did any of these favorable events take place for Libya, where currently it is slowly making its journey to international normality. Why should the approach be any different for Iran?

---

[13] Joseph, 2.

[14] Office of the Press Secretary, "US Eases Economic Embargo Against Libya," April 23, 2004, http://www.whitehouse.gov/news/releases/2004/04/print/20040423-9.html (accessed February 13, 2008).

Chapter Seven

7. EVALUATING FOREIGN POLICY APPROACHES

The Regionally Appropriate Saudi Approach

The Kingdom deals with the Islamic Republic just as many other states deal with its regional competitor—by attempting to create a regional balance of power. The distinguishing features of the Muslim Arab and Persian culture makes the situation in the Middle East very unique. Saudi Arabia views the region predominantly with a sectarian and Arab lens, but acknowledges and respects the Persian dimension in the region. However, the Kingdom incorporates its shared Arab values and understanding of Islam into its employment of soft power to reduce Iran's influences within the region. And with a non-threatening disposition and a willingness to maintain open lines of communication, Saudi Arabia pursues regional stability through mutually respectful and culturally sensitive engagement.

Saudi General Foreign Policy Principles

The Kingdom offers very little insight into its intended policy outcomes. Its often secretive approach does manifest itself in subtle but defining ways. Saudi Arabia's past and present dealings with Iran falls somewhat in line with what the country advocates is its foreign policy positions. The Kingdom's Ministry of Foreign Affairs summarizes its foreign policy based on its particular self-categorized "circles"— in order of importance, the Gulf Circle, the Arab Circle, the Islamic Circle and the International Circle. The following principles specified below are necessary in understanding the Saudi approach to Iran:

- Value the principles of sovereignty and non interference in the internal affairs of any country. In addition, reject any attempt of others to interfere in Her internal affairs.
- Work out for international peace and justice, and reject the use of power and violence or any actions that threaten the international peace or lead to the building up of injustice and autocracy.
- Defend Arab and Islamic issues in the international arena through continuous support by all political, diplomatic, and economic means.
- Nonalignment and rejection of disputes that threaten international security and peace, and respect the right of people for self determination and their lawful rights for self-defense.[1]

Saudi Arabia behaves in a way that respects the borders and sovereignty of Iran, for it never interferes in Iran's domestic affairs, even when Iran's political system struggles for an identity. King Abdullah publicly received Iranian National Security Advisor Larijani in Riyadh in January 2007, where he advised Larijani that Iran should be careful to observe limits in its dealings with outside powers, but at the same time assured the Iranians that Saudi Arabia had not joined a bloc against them nor would Saudi Arabia support any efforts to interfere in Iranian domestic politics.[2]

Additionally, King Abdullah invested much of his reputation and credibility with his quest for international peace through an Arab-Israeli Peace Initiative. This placed Saudi Arabia as a contender of the Iranian support to Hezbollah and HAMAS but fulfilled the Kingdom's goal of striving for international peace and justice. Proclaiming Saudi loyalty to the Sunni community of Iraq affected the Iranian-backed Shiite majority

---

[1] Kingdom of Saudi Arabia, Ministry of Foreign Affairs, "Kingdom Foreign Policy— The foreign policy of the Kingdom of Saudi Arabia," 3, http://www.mofa.gov.sa/Detail.asp?InSectionID=3989&InNewsItemID=34645 (accessed February 14, 2008).

[2] F. Gregory Gause III, "Saudi Arabia: Iraq, Iran, the Regional Power Balance, and the Sectarian Question," *Strategic Insights,* VI, no. 2 (March 2007), 4, http://www.ccc.nps.navy.mil/si/2007/Mar/gauseMar07.pdf (accessed January 10, 2008).

but is seen as justified in order to champion the self-determination rights of the Sunni people.

Saudi Foreign Policy Principles of the Inner Circles

While those general principles mentioned previously guide Saudi foreign policy in a manner that affects Iran, the Kingdom simultaneously employs the following principles of the Gulf Circle and Arab Circle, which use soft power to strengthen Saudi Arabia's position in the region:

- Strengthen cooperation between the Kingdom and the member states of the GCC in different political, economical, security, social, cultural fields and others, through deepening and consolidating relations and ties among member states.
- The inevitable connection between Arab-nationalism and Islam.
- The necessity of Arab solidarity, together with coordination among the Arab countries with the aim to unify Arab stances and utilize all potentials and resources of Arab countries to serve the Arab interests.
- Commitment to the principle of Arab brotherhood through offering all types of support and assistance.[3]

The blood relations, historical connections, and unique geographical neighborhood that bring the Arab Gulf states together compels the Saudis to develop organizations like the GCC. It increased its economic influence through the creation of a common market and its proposals for an enhanced military capability with the expansion of its Peninsula Shield military force benefits the GCC's relative position within the region.

Implementation of current Saudi foreign policy involves constant dialogue. Cordial engagements and invitations for senior Iranian officials to different conferences and assemblies demonstrate a commitment to diplomacy. Their mutual concern for

---

[3] Kingdom of Saudi Arabia, Ministry of Foreign Affairs, 1-2.

instability in Iraq equates to regional conferences between leaders such as the one held in March 2007.[4] Leadership at all levels, such as those that participated in the January 2008 Iran-Saudi Arabia parliamentary friendship group, seeks to deepen bilateral ties. This openness reinforces the old ties between the two countries, as they exchanged political and parliamentary delegations to bolster interests of the two countries and the Islamic world and to destroy disunity and religious conflicts in the Islamic countries.[5] This friendship group sends a message to the world that there is an apparent sincere and brotherly behavior between two countries willing to peacefully coexist.

With the internationally sensitive topic of Iran's nuclear development, Saudi Arabia remains relatively neutral. The Kingdom respects Iran's right as a state to develop a nuclear capability, so long as its programs are for peaceful purposes such as an alternative source of energy. This type of position enables the Kingdom to possibly pursue a similar path, as introduced during a visit from French President Nicolas Sarkozy in January 2008, when he proposed to send a team from the Atomic Energy Commission to look into building a civilian nuclear energy program in Saudi Arabia that may include a transfer of technology.[6] While the Kingdom does oppose Iran's nuclear weapons program, it cautiously approaches this issue due to a lack of definitive evidence that a nuclear weapons program is actually under construction, preventing King Abdullah from

---

[4] Agencies, "Iran and Saudi pledge friendship," Al Jazeera, March 3, 2007, http://english.aljazeera.net/NR/exeres/D4EEF783-C1CE-467F-824C-DD67943B2255.htm (accessed February 15, 2008).

[5] Islamic Repbulic News Agency. "Iran-Saudi Arabian parliamentary friendship group hold meeting in Riyadh," January 27, 2008, http://www2.irna.ir/en/news/view/menu-234/0801271690004753.htm (accessed February 15, 2008).

[6] Kumaran Ira, "France obtains energy deals, establishes first military base in Persian Gulf," World Socialist Web Site, http://www.wewe.org/articles/2008/jan2008/sark-j24.shtml (accessed February 15, 2008).

having to emphatically object to Iran's nuclear aspirations. [7] Conversations pertaining to nuclear capabilities may remain friendly unless competent authority assesses a nuclear proliferation within Iran.

The Kingdom's commitment to communication with the Islamic Republic of Iran even extends beyond its own sovereignty as it has leveraged its influence within the GCC to engage with Iranian President Ahmadinejad in the December 2007 GCC summit. GCC states have lacked a consensus on how to deal with Iran. Some states like Qatar and the United Arab Emirates have sought to balance their relations with the U.S. and Iran. Concerned with its economic well-being, Oman opts not to engage in geopolitics. Kuwait and Bahrain maintain a more hard-line attitude towards Iran. Collectively, however, the GCC's invitation to the Iranian President is representative of Saudi Arabia's very pragmatic approach of engaging Iran rather than leaving it to its own devices. [8]

The GCC's engagement with Iran symbolizes Saudi Arabia's commitment to Arab solidarity, a cultural aspect that is practically non-existent elsewhere. Saudi Arabia purposely distances itself from the U.S. especially when it deals with Iran. Motivated by its innate responsibility as the self-perceived leader of the Arab world and its notion of having the capacity to deal with Iran without non-regional support, the Kingdom casually discusses Middle East issues such as Iran with the U.S. only in general terms. Besides the Kingdom's religious and cultural connectivity to the Middle Eastern states, there is still enduring bitterness resulting from the period after 9/11. While fifteen out of the

---

[7] National Intelligence Council, *National Intelligence Estimate – Iran: Nuclear Intentions and Capabilities,* Prepared by the Office of the Director of National Intelligence, November 2007, 6, http://www.dni.gov/press_releases/200712013_release.pdf (accessed March 1, 2008).

[8] Strategic Forecasting, Inc., "Iran: An Invitation to the Gulf Cooperation Council," November 29, 2007, under "Summary," http://www.stratfor.com/analysis/iran_invitation_gulf_cooperation_council (accessed February 15, 2008).

nineteen perpetrators of the attacks on the World Trade Center and the Pentagon were Saudis,[9] the Bush administration did not convincingly separate the Islamic extremists from the rest of the Saudi community, which created an international distaste for Sunni fundamentalism, a crisis that King Abdullah had to overcome.

The Islamic community perceives Western support unfavorably, for the Bush administration did little to separate Islam from terror. American approval of Saudi Arabia's policy toward Iran gives the appearance that the Kingdom is merely acting as a puppet of the West. The Kingdom already struggles with the appearance of being a Zionistic state supporter with King Abdullah's Arab-Israeli Peace Initiative. U.S. sponsorship of the Kingdom's policy towards Iran would only further increase the overall Iranian Shiite influence that is growing with Hamas, Hezbollah, the Iraqi Shiites, and other Shiite communities. Therefore, Saudi Arabia does not seek American acceptance of its Iran policy because it would make the Islamic Republic appear to be the lone Muslim power willing to stand up to the Western infidels.

The Kingdom's Ministry of Foreign Affairs policy outline did not mention the perceived necessity to counter the spread of Shiite influence in the region. Not overtly recognizing this need allows for an angle the Saudis can use to counterbalance Iranian influence. In areas where three potential civil wars that are likely to destabilize and polarize the Middle East— referring to the sectarian strife between Shiites and Sunnis in Iraq, the political unrest in Lebanon caused by disagreement between Hezbollah and the Lebanese government, and the violence between HAMAS and Fatah in the West Bank

---

[9]Aarts and Nonneman, 47.

and Gaza Strip[10]—Saudi Arabia's diplomacy efforts may undercut Iranian soft power influences.

The effort continues at home with the Sunni Arabs resident in the oil-rich Hasa province and others, where the government placates this minority community.

> The Saudi government has been on a minor, but in the Saudi context significant, charm offensive toward its own Shi'a minority for a number of years. The Saudi Shi'a leader Hassan al-Safar was publicly invited to participate in the King's "National Dialogue" initiative which began in 2003 . . . Municipal council elections in 2005 allowed Saudi Shi'a to elect representatives for the first time in decades to help manage their cities . . . Perhaps most importantly from a symbolic standpoint, Saudi Shi'a for the past three years (2004-2007) have been able to commemorate the Shi'a feast of Ashura publicly. Such public commemorations have been banned for decades, and are particularly offensive to hard-line salafis from the Wahhabi tradition."[11]

It is evident that the cultural dimension of sectarian identities is a large component of the Kingdom's regional balance of power politics, coupled with its emphasis on the principles identified for those of the Inner Circles. In terms of implementation, Saudi Arabia pursues a foreign policy in a nuanced rather than overtly confrontational way.

The Ineffective American Isolation of Iran

What is Isolation?

President Bush's methods of foreign policy with Islamic Republic of Iran, from the public statements to the unilateral and multilateral sanctions, attempt to isolate this nation. A strategy of containment confronts the opposition at strategic points of conflict and holds them there. Unfortunately, following this course, the initiative is given to the

---

[10] Bahgat, 49.

[11] Gause, 4.

opposition and containment becomes a policy of reaction.[12] Henry Kissinger calls containment a "doctrine of perpetual struggle,"[13] where the goal is "the age-old American dream of a peace achieved by the conversion of the adversary."[14]

The Axis of Evil Speech

In his State of the Union Address to Congress on January 29, 2002, President Bush used the expression, the Axis of Evil, to include Iraq, Iran and North Korea: "States like these, and their terrorist allies, constitute an Axis of Evil, arming to threaten the peace of the world. By seeking weapons of mass destruction, these regimes pose a grave and growing danger."[15] This creative metaphor had the intention of giving the international community a new view of the world.[16]

> In this respect the Axis of Evil metaphor was a kind of cognitive breakthrough, an effort to restructure the international system as it was in the 1930s—an attempt to see the world through the eyes of that period. Recalling the Second World War, the Axis Powers are evil, and the implication is that something must be done about them. If you find the metaphor to be compelling, then you must act. In fact, metaphor sanctions actions and helps to build goals. [17]

---

[12] Jerr L. Mraz and John P. McCallen, "Dual Containment in the Persian Gulf: Strategic Considerations and Policy Options" (master's thesis, Naval Postgraduate School, 1996), 41, http://stinet.dtic.mil/cgi-bin/GetTRDoc?AD=ADA311402&Location=U2$doc=GetTRDoc.pdf (accessed February 16, 2008).

[13] Henry Kissinger, "Reflections on Containment," *Foreign Affairs*, 73, No. 3 (May/June 1994): 122, http://ezproxy6.ndu.edu/login?url=http://search.ebscohost.com/login.aspx?direct=true&db=afh&AN=9409082432&site=ehost-live (accessed February 13, 2008).

[14] Kissinger, 120.

[15] George W. Bush, "State of the Union Address" (January 29, 2002), http://www.whitehouse.gov/new/releases/2002/01/20020129-11.htm (accessed February 15, 2008).

[16] Paul Ricoeur, *Rule of Metaphor* (Toronto: University of Toronto Press, 1977), 99.

[17] George Lakoff and Mark Johnson, *Metaphors We Live By* (Chicago: University of Chicago Press, 1980), 142.

However, while the metaphor may have attempted to restructure the way the West viewed Iran, it also may have restructured the way the Iranians view the world, and themselves.[18] The Bush administration appeared to have no idea what impact its words would have. Condoleezza Rice, Bush's national security advisor at the time even said, "what is funny about it is that [the phrase] didn't really catch my eye." For many Iranians, however, the remark was devastating.[19]

Interviews conducted by analysts with members of the Iranian oppositional elite suggest that the American warning to Iran embedded in the Axis of Evil speech had multiple domestic impacts. The speech gave conservatives pause and resulted in greater national unity and alienation of reformers. The reformers met the conservatives half-way, with a suddenly decreased enthusiasm for normalization of relations with a country that had betrayed, threatened, and insulted them in this manner. The metaphor mistakenly targeted the entire country, not just the leadership, and it failed to differentiate the "evil" leaders from the others who live in the country.[20] While President Bush has since stopped using the metaphor, it nevertheless halted the nascent dialogue in 2002 that was secretly occurring between government officials during the early stages of Operation Enduring Freedom (OEF).[21] The politically savvy Iranian conservatives continue to propagate the metaphor to their advantage.

> The right wing of the Revolutionary Guard affiliated with Mahmud Ahmadinejad likes to repeat this metaphor as an example of what satanic forces the U.S. represents. This is an example of how a sender of any given message can lose

---

[18] Daniel Heradstveit and G. Matthew Bonham, "What the Axis of Evil Metaphor Did to Iran," *The Middle East Journal*, 61, no. 3 (Summer 2007): 421.

[19] Slavin, 12.

[20] Heradstveit and Bonham, 437-438.

[21] Slavin, 198-199.

control over its further use. New senders can resend it in a form that is quite contrary to what the original sender intended. It is not even necessary for the new senders to create new meaning, because the changing political context has already given it new meaning.[22]

American and Iranian Self-Images

While the metaphor may have assisted in the revitalization of the Islamic Republic's sense of nationalism, a consideration of Iranian and American self-image reveals a hidden irony. The self-image of each nation appears diametrically opposed on the surface, but a deeper look at the roots of the self-image indicates that a sense of "special providence" forms the core of national identity for both Iran and the U.S.[23] Scholar Walter Russell Mead identifies:

> That special providence at the nexus of four domestic source pools of American power: concerns over the protection of commerce; the maintenance of the nation's democratic-republican forms of governance; preservation and promotion of America's populist values and military might; and finally, America's "moral principle."[24]

Meanwhile,

> The origins of Iran's 'special providence' are found in the requiem for a more splendid past—in fact, three interconnected pasts. The first past can be found by tracing Iran's genealogy back to the Persian Empire, historically one of the world greatest superpowers with a monotheistic religion, rich civilization, vast army, elite forms of governance and a wide and expansive territory. A second past is found in Islam, in Iran's history as the only Shia Muslim state in the world. In this regard, Iranian identity is based on both a positive sense of uniqueness and a negative sense of isolation. A third, more recent past is a reality built upon the sense of empire lost and isolation intensified through an incursion and imposition of European modernity on the Iranian state.[25]

---

[22] Heradstveit and Bonham, 438.

[23] Wilson, 98.

[24] Kenneth M. Pollack, *The Persian Puzzle: The Conflict Between Iran and America* (New York: Random House, 2004), 3-26.

[25] Wilson, 100.

The two nations see themselves as powerful and influential nations, with one perceiving

to dominate the world and the other perceiving to be once fallen but back on the rise;

both perspectives appear to be narrow-minded in its appreciation of the other's status.

When placed in an appropriate historical context, the current American foreign

policy does not exercise the sensitivity that history suggests.

> Where America's brief historic sense of self (232 years) reveals a story of progress from backwater beginning to contemporary world hegemon, Iran's story begins long ago from regal beginnings. While America's self identity seems to tell a progressive story, until most recently, Iran's sense of self might be perceived as a long fall from grace . . . For Iran, there is an ever-present goal to recapture its past grandeur and providence, believed to have been unfairly taken away. For America, the dominant idea is one of a special providence uniquely earned and presently under increasing challenge from the Islamic Republic of Iran . . . The U.S. objective is perceived as an interference that has robbed Iran of its own special providence on several occasions throughout history. Conversely, the peace and stability that the Islamic Republic of Iran seeks—a natural and righteous return to a lost past when Iran was the regional hegemon—in viewed by the United States and the West as a direct affront to its own presence and aspirations.[26]

From this Iranian perspective, the U.S. is merely in its way and is not deserving of being

a hindrance to its growing dominance.

> Most of the history framing the current relationship between the United States and Iran within each country covers only the past twenty-five to thirty years. The recounting of this history is plagued by hyper-inflated rhetoric and is devoid of much of the aforementioned ideational baseline to that relationship. We are all too familiar with the irreconcilable animosities that have characterized the story of the American-Iranian relationship over the past thirty years. For Americans, the narrative is one that was born during the 1979 hostage crisis. For Iranians, it is a tale that began at least twenty-six years earlier with the CIA-supported coup against the Iranian prime minister, Mohammed Mossadeq, and America's hand in the reinstatement of the shah to the Peacock Throne.[27]

---

[26] Wilson, 101.

[27] Pollack, 26.

"Amid this narrative, most Iranians and Americans have limited their understanding of the other to animosities and rhetorical saber-rattling."[28]

From these self-image perspectives, both nations feel justified with their actions of pursuing whatever it wishes to pursue. Relative to their own understanding of the world, as seen from their own particular lens, both act irrespective of each other's perceived national convictions.

The American Approach to the Nuclear Issue

With use of what can be argued as an inappropriate metaphor, President Bush's inconsistent dealings with states that pursued WMD programs only instills confidence in Iran. After Libya surrendered nuclear equipment in 2003, the U.S. reestablished full diplomatic relations with Libya two years later, even though it was still ruled by the eccentric and thoroughly undemocratic Moammar Gadhafi. Iran, a country of seventy million situated at a strategically important choke point of the Persian Gulf in no way compares to Libya, a nation of only five million people with limited U.S. strategic value.[29] In the case of Libya, the measures employed by the U.S. were successful and communicated to the Islamic Republic that the U.S. will open relations if they do the same. The experience of other proliferators, namely, North Korea, sent different signals to Iran.

> Confronted in late 2002 by the Bush administration about a clandestine effort to acquire parts for a uranium enrichment program, North Korea withdrew from the NPT and kicked out IAEA monitors in early 2003. It then resumed operation of a nuclear complex that churned out plutonium and amassed enough fuel for perhaps a dozen bombs. The Bush administration at first refused to talk to North Korea,

---

[28] Wilson, 101.

[29] Slavin, 35.

then joined multinational talks and agreed in February 2007 to provide economic and diplomatic benefits in return for North Korea's promise to give up the nuclear program again. The message to Iran was clear: Become a nuclear power and no one will dare attack you; accelerate your efforts to become a weapons state and other countries will offer you many inducements to give up or limit your program."[30]

Surely, Iran holds at least equal status with North Korea, who struggles to barely maintain most facets of its national power. Therefore, the Iranian leadership may argue that the U.S. will eventually concede and engage in serious dialogue.

Direct U.S. engagement took place with another nation with increasing nuclear ambitions—India—and the U.S.-India deal[31] even violated the nonproliferation treaty which forbids the five acknowledged nuclear weapons powers (Russia, China, France, Britain, and the U.S.) from undertaking activities that could assist other countries' nuclear weapons programs:

> A U.S. offer of civilian nuclear cooperation with India in 2006 also encouraged Iran to believe it could have nuclear prowess and foreign trade and investment, too. India had exploded its first nuclear device in 1974 and carried out further testing in 1998 but was offered absolution by Washington after it developed a lucrative economic relationship with the U.S.[32]

Henry Sokolski, who heads the Nonproliferation Policy Education Center, a think tank in Washington, explained that the U.S. deal with India convinced Iran that it was not a question of rights but of "being picked on" because it was not friendly to the U.S. and was perceived as weak.[33]

---

[30] Slavin, 33.

[31] Esther Pan and Jayshree Bajoria, "The U.S.-India Nuclear Deal," Council on Foreign Relations, February 7, 2008, http://www.cfr.org/publication/9663/ (accessed February 13, 2008).

[32] Slavin, 34.

[33] Slavin, 34.

Lastly, a perceived double standard of ignoring Israel's officially unacknowledged but widely believed possession of several hundred nuclear weapons as well as the nuclear programs of India and Pakistan, which, like Israel, never joined the NPT, irritated Iranian leadership. In 2006, Iranian National Security Advisor Larijani accused the U.S. of using international treaties and organizations to punish countries that chose not to follow U.S. views, emphasizing that a superpower such as the U.S. must respect others and not expect others to be its servants.[34] As Iran's former foreign minister remarked in 2004 referring to the U.S. acceptance of Israel's nuclear weapons, "it is really unbelievable why Americans make themselves the yardstick for being right and wrong. Who has given them this right?"[35]

The Bush administration underestimated the sense of nationalism of the Islamic Republic. The Iranians are a people who pull together when threatened or attacked—very much like Americans. Iran's clerical leadership, however much despised by so many of its people, is not set to topple at the first hint of a crisis. Instead, it could count on consolidating its rule—just as the Ayatollah Khomenei used Saddam Hussein's invasion to solidify his power.[36] As the nearby states of Afghanistan and Iraq which once threatened Iran's security underwent serious change with the removal of the tyrannical regimes of the Taliban and Saddam Hussein respectively, Iran intensified its focus on defending itself. A nuclear weapons capability, of which Iran is suspected of pursuing, is an alternative form of defense. "If Iran is pursuing weapons, the action is at

---

[34] Slavin, 34.

[35] Slavin, 35.

[36] Robert E. Hunter, "Time to Talk to Iran," RAND Corporation, http://www.rand.org/commentary/042606WP.html (accessed February 13, 2008).

least in part a response to Iranian fears of a possible U.S. military attack patterned after the invasion of Iraq."[37]

While the Islamic Republic justifies its pursuit of a nuclear capability to complement its energy resources, the "Bush administration officials argue that Iran's nuclear program must be a cover for bomb making."[38]   However, Iran's concerns are legitimate:

> A review of objective facts would establish Iran's need for alternative sources of energy, including nuclear energy. According to a recently released study by the National Academy of Science, "Iran's energy demand growth has exceeded its supply growth," and therefore, "Iran's oil export will decline," or even "could go to zero within 12-19 years."[39]

The study acknowledges that Iran's need for nuclear power is "genuine, because Iran relies on . . . proceeds from oil exports for most revenues, and adds, "will substitute for the power now generated by petroleum, thus, freeing petroleum for export."[40]   The same Western governments that are questioning the feasibility of Iran's nuclear energy program today, were actually supporting and competing for shares in the program over forty years ago, when Iran's population and energy demands were far lower than current levels and export far higher.[41]   Supporters of Iran's nuclear energy program may argue that the 2007 NIE of Iran reconfirms the peaceful purposes of Iran's nuclear development

---

[37] Robert E. Hunter, "Grand Strategy for the Middle East," RAND Corporation, http://www.rand.org/commentary/111906SDUT.html (accessed February 13, 2008).

[38] Mohammad Javad Zarif, "Tackling the U.S.-Iran Crisis: The Need for a Paradigm Shift.," *Journal of International Affairs* 60, no. 2 (Spring/Summer 2007): 78.

[39] International Monetary Fund, Islamic Republic of Iran: Statistical Appendix, IMF Country Report 04/307 (Washington, D.C.: International Monetary Fund, 2004).

[40] Roger Stern, "The Iranian Petroleum Crisis and United States National Security," *Proceeding of the National Academy of Sciences* 104, no. 1377 (January 2, 2007), http://www.ncbi.nlm.nih.gov/pubmed/17190820 (accessed January 31, 2008).

[41] Zarif, 78.

and research and should thus not be constantly interrupted or blocked by the international community.

In Larger Context – Dual Containment, an Invalid Policy

In examining the threats posed by both Iran and Iraq, one will notice that with the fall of Saddam's regime, it marked the end of an era of foreign policy. President Bill Clinton devised a strategy that Martin Indyk, then top Middle East advisor on the White House National Security Council, dubbed "dual containment."[42] This policy sought to isolate and stabilize both Iran and Iraq. Dual containment achieved success provided that the regimes in Iran and Iraq despised the U.S. more than each other. Essentially, each contained the other, thereby minimizing U.S. effort to sustain the process for more than a decade. The invasion of Afghanistan in 2001 and Iraq in 2003 brought about the removal of the principal props from the dual containment strategy without changing the underlying policy.[43] Iran was left to its own devices, and with some coincidental assistance from the U.S., became stronger.

The Bush administration declared war on Iran's greatest regional foes: the Sunni fundamentalist Taliban regime in Afghanistan that harbored al-Qaeda and also murdered Farsi-speaking Afghan Shiites and Iranian diplomats; and the secular Baathist dictatorship of Iraq's Saddam Hussein, which had invaded Iran in 1980 and was responsible for the deaths of three hundred thousand Iranians.[44] The removal of the

---

[42] Martin Indyk, Graham Fuller, Anthony H. Cordesman, and Phebe Marr, "Symposium on Dual Containment: U.S. Policy Toward Iran and Iraq, *Middle East Policy* 3, no. 1 (1994), 1.

[43] James Dobbins, "My Enemy's Enemy," RAND Corporation, http://www.rand.org/commentary/022707IHT.html (accessed February 13, 2008).

[44] Slavin, 11.

Taliban regime and the installation of members of the Northern Alliance made conditions extensively better for the Iranians. The Islamic Republic supported the Northern Alliance against its struggle with the Taliban years before U.S. lent its support. The Northern Alliance was an amalgam of fighters from groups other than the Taliban's ethnic Pushtun factions, including Tajik Shiite Muslims.[45]

With another pro-Iranian regime in Iraq that has long received Iranian support, there are no regional counterweights to Iran. Co-dependence between the leaderships of Kabul and Tehran as well as Baghdad and Tehran will exist long after the U.S. departs the region. As a result, neither the Afghan nor the Iraqi government may ever welcome any efforts by the U.S. to isolate Iran, contain its influence or destabilize its regime. Between Afghanistan and Iraq, the U.S. may not ever find an ally that would be willing to go against their powerful and friendly Iranian neighbor.[46] Regional partners loyal to the U.S., particularly ones so strategically close to the Islamic Republic, would compound Iran's security concerns; without an Iraqi and Afghan pledge to the U.S., Bush loses leveraging capability in the region.

Cultural Considerations Overlooked

In some respects, the Bush administration demonstrates a deficiency in considering that the Islamic Republic of Iran represents a proud and historic Persian heritage, and not just a tyrannical regime that supports terror:

> More than five hundred years before the birth of Jesus Christ, a Persian king, Cyrus the Great, build an empire that stretched from present-day Turkey to

---

[45] Slavin, 198.

[46] James Dobbins, "My Enemy's Enemy," RAND Corporation, http://www.rand.org/commentary/022707IHT.html (accessed February 13, 2008).

Afghanistan. The empire crumbled, but Iranian civilization triumphed. It absorbed waves of invaders from Greeks to Mongols to Turks and Arabs, changing the invaders more than it was itself transformed.[47]

They are a resilient nation that withstood an aggressor during the eight year war with Iraq and now years of sanctions imposed by the U.S. More importantly,

> The public response in Iran to the September 11 attacks shows how different Iran, a non-Arab country, is from much of the rest of the Muslim world. While many Arabs celebrated what they saw as a long-deserved blow against the prime supporter of Israel, many Iranians held spontaneous candlelit demonstrations in sympathy with the U.S. victims. With links to a diaspora of nearly a million people in the United States, little regard for Arabs, and a cultural appreciation for innocent victims of violence, Iranians instinctively felt a connection with those who died at the World Trade Center, the Pentagon and on the plane that crashed in Pennsylvania.[48]

It appears as though there is a populace in Iran that is sympathetic to the U.S., one that is somewhat receptive to ideals consistent to a Western society. "Outside and inside the Iranian regime there is tremendous ambivalence about America. No other country is so fixated on the United States. No other foreign government so aspires to and fears a U.S. embrace."[49]

This populace has a profound impact on the Supreme Leader Ayatollah Khamenei. He responds to the views of the domestic populace and values the strength of the people of Iran. When necessary, Khamenei will swiftly intervene in the execution of policy, particularly when it concerns his people, and even when his actions may be in direct opposition to the actions of other Iranian leaders. For example, in January 2008, a harsh winter compelled the Supreme Leader to reverse a decision by President

---

[47] Slavin, 13.

[48] Slavin, 11.

[49] Slavin, 9.

Ahmadinejad, ordering him to implement a law supplying natural gas to remote villages that were intentionally neglected for budgetary reasons. Obviously, the Supreme Leader was concerned for the welfare of the Iranian people. However, Khamenei also recognized the discontent of his people with Ahmadinejad as the winter progressed and Iran's recent decline in the agriculture and housing markets.[50] Khamenei's intervention sends a message to the Iranian President that the nation was somewhat displeased with the economic direction. His intervention also suggests that the Iranian populace has the power to drive policy and a population obsessed with the U.S. may be a hidden blessing.

Sanctions and pressure against Iran may satisfy some American domestic constituencies or settle some old scores. However, the U.S. is on a disillusioned path of progress, resulting from a lack of cultural sensitivity and understanding. At the current pace, the U.S. will more likely unravel the non-proliferation regime, exacerbate tension, perpetuate the enemy paradigm and lead to unwanted—even accidental—escalations.[51]

---

[50] Associated Press, "Khamenei reverses gas cut decision by Ahmadinejad," *Gulf News,* January 21, 2008, http://archive.gulfnews.com/articles/08/01/22/10183770.html (accessed February 28, 2008).

[51] Zarif, 87-88.

Chapter Eight

8. RECOMMENDED U.S. FOREIGN POLICY ADJUSTMENTS

U.S. Opportunities Missed

A non-unified body of foreign policy makers constituted a lack of dialogue that has prevailed during the current administration. Secretary of State Colin Powell was open to new approaches with Iran at the start of the Bush administration but found himself stymied from the start in his efforts to implement a traditional Republican realist policy toward so-called rogue states, facing fierce opposition from Vice President Dick Cheney, and former Secretary of Defense Donald Rumsfeld.[1]

State Department officials attempted to send a few positive signals to Tehran but met opposition during the beginning of the Bush term. Richard Haass, Powell's director of policy planning, attempted to reduce the renewal of the Iran Libya Sanctions Act to two years but lost to the Republican-led Congress, and tried unsuccessfully to get the administration to drop its longtime opposition to Iran applying to join the WTO. Haass reasoned that these modest gestures would send positive signals, a way to bring about regime modification, but although there was sympathy for his position at the upper levels of the State Department, it was not shared elsewhere in the administration.[2]

The U.S. tragedy of the September 11 attacks and a compassionate Iranian nation created a strategic opportunity that ultimately U.S. decision makers failed to recognize. The Iranians consciously cooperated on Afghanistan, not making it contingent upon a change in U.S. policy, believing that their actions would automatically have altered the

---

[1] Tom Regan, "Report: Cheney Rejected Iran's Offer of Concessions in 2003," *The Christian Science Monitor- csmonitor.com*, January 18, 2007, http://www.csmonitor.com/2007/0118/p99s01-duts.html (accessed February 15, 2008).

[2] Slavin, 196-197.

nature of Iran-U.S. relations. Besides the close ties with leaders of most of the anti-

Taliban factions and being the major supporter to the Northern Alliance, Iran played a

critical role in the diplomatic arena, helping to construct a broad-based government to

replace the Taliban regime, even suggesting that the draft communiqué call for

democracy in Afghanistan and declare that the new government should not harbor

terrorists.[3] James Dobbins, the Bush administration's special envoy for Afghanistan

applauded Iran for its active role and for being the most helpful delegation.[4]

Much of this activity remained under wraps. U.S. and Iranian diplomats met

numerous times between 2001 and 2003 under United Nations (UN) auspices, alternating

between Geneva and Paris, and discussions ranged from Iranian advice on targeting

within Afghanistan to the handling of al-Qaeda fugitives. Iranian cooperation went so far

as the provision of two hundred copies of Arab passports for those who fled Afghanistan

and the deportation of refugees mostly back to their home countries. [5]

Quiet cooperation continued despite the dreaded "Axis of Evil" metaphor and

when discussions began including a possible invasion of Iraq, deputy foreign minister for

Iran, Mohammad Javad Zarif expressed support for the U.S. attack on Iraq so long as it

was not intended as a launching pad against Iran. Despite all the Iranian cooperation, one

request was left unfulfilled—rather than treating the Mujahedin e-Khalq (MEK), the anti-

regime Iranian group that had been given refuge by Saddam Hussein, as enemy

combatants like the Iranian diplomats requested, the U.S. military instead signed a truce

with the MEK and put its members under U.S. protection. The U.S. reasoned that there

---

[3] James Dobbins, "Time to Deal with Iran," *Washington Post,* May 6, 2004.

[4] Slavin, 198-199.

[5] Slavin, 198-199.

were not only enough troops to deal with the MEK, but also Zalmay Khalilzad, a senior member of the White House National Security Council, complained that the Iranians did not properly deal with al-Qaeda detainees by turning them over to the U.S., Afghanistan, or Arab governments.[6] Nevertheless, as cooperative with Afghanistan as the Iranians were, the U.S. did not reciprocate even with this single, legitimate request.

As previously mentioned, U.S.-Iran collaboration was transparent to the international community. Americans who participated in the discussions that occurred in Geneva and Paris did not take notes or prepare written cables. This hidden diplomacy was done in order to reinforce the perception that the U.S. can do it alone and working with a terrorist state like Iran would appear as a victory for al-Qaeda. The Bush administration did not want to be placed in a situation where it would have to be grateful to the Iranians or recognize the legitimacy of the Iranian government. Regardless of the circumstances, Iranian diplomats sought more ambitious initiatives in 2003, which encompassed comprehensive talks between the U.S. and Iran. Prepared by Iran's then ambassador to France, Sadegh Kharrazi, in consultation with the then Swiss ambassador in Tehran, Tim Guldimann, a statesman well briefed on U.S. concerns, the agenda listed Iranian and U.S. aims for negotiations, including all issues of major importance to the two sides.[7]

After Zarif, Iran's deputy foreign minister, refined the preliminary document, the proposal for the comprehensive talks had something for everyone. This authoritative initiative had the support of then-President Mahammad Khatami and Supreme Leader Ali

---

[6] Slavin, 203.

[7] Slavin, 204-205.

Khamenei. Addressed to President Bush, the Near East Bureau of the State Department

received the document shortly after the 2003 Iraq invasion:

> The document lists a series of Iranian aims for the talks, such as ending sanctions,
> full access to peaceful nuclear technology and a recognition of its "legitimate
> security interests." Iran agreed to put a series of U.S. aims on the agenda,
> including full cooperation on nuclear safeguards, "decisive action" against
> terrorists, coordination in Iraq, ending "material support" for Palestinian militias
> and accepting the Saudi initiative for a two-state solution in the Israeli-Palestinian
> conflict.[8]

> The U.S., for its part, would accept 'a dialogue in mutual respect' about Iran's
> concerns, among them a halt in 'hostile behavior' toward Iran, the end of U.S.
> economic sanctions, access to peaceful nuclear technology, a clampdown on the
> MEK, and 'recognition of Iran's legitimate security interests in the region.'[9]

"The document also laid out an agenda for negotiations, with steps to be achieved at a

first meeting and the development of negotiating road maps on disarmament, terrorism

and economic cooperation."[10] This offer was not taken seriously at the highest levels of

the Bush administration, particularly with Dick Cheney and Donald Rumsfeld. After a

terrorist bombing in Riyadh killed eight Americans and 26 Saudis on May 12, 2003,

Rumsfeld convinced President Bush that senior al-Qaeda officials responsible for the

bombing were. Despite a lack of evidence, Rumsfeld and Cheney persuaded Bush to

cancel the May 21 meeting with Iranian officials and in a masterstroke, they had shut

---

[8] Glenn Kessler, "In 2003, U.S. Spurned Iran's Offer of Dialogue," *The Washington Post,* June 18, 2006, A16, http://www.washingtonpost.com/wp-dyn/content/article/2006/06/17/AR006061700727_pf.html (accessed February 29, 2008).

[9] Slavin, 205.

[10] Kessler, A16.

down the only diplomatic avenue available for communication with Iran and convinced

Bush that Iran was on the same side as al-Qaeda.[11]

U.S. failure to restore law and order to the cities of Iraq counteracted with the

initial awe of Iranian officials in the speed with which the Americans moved during the

invasion of Iraq.

> Rice's belief—and that of President Bush and Vice President Cheney—in the
> rightness of the Iraq war and the beneficial impact it would have on the rest of the
> Middle East led the Bush administration to miss or mishandle repeated
> opportunities to reach out to Iran . . . By the time the administration offered in
> May 2006 to talk to Iran about its nuclear program . . . Iran had been so
> emboldened by other U.S. policies that it felt little pressure or inclination to
> accept.[12]

Iran was further motivated not to cooperate with the U.S. by the State Department's move

to solicit proposals from "educational institutions, humanitarian groups, non-government

organizations and individuals inside Iran to support the advancement of democracy and

human rights." This violated the 1981 accord that freed U.S. diplomatic hostages and

promised that the U.S. would not "intervene directly or indirectly, politically or militarily,

in Iran's internal affairs."[13]

Identifying the need to adjust policy, the U.S. eventually decided in May 2006 to

participate in talks with Iran, along with Russia, China, Britain, France, and Germany,

and augment the European's previous offer of economic and diplomatic goodies, but only

if Iran suspended its uranium enrichment program. The policy shift translated into tough

talk once again, as Rice proclaimed that Iran had two paths to choose from—integration

---

[11] Gareth Porter, "How a 2003 secret overture from Tehran might have led to a deal on Iran's nuclear capacity—if the Bush administration hadn't rebuffed it," *The American Prospect,* May 21, 2006, http://www.prospect.org/cs/articles?articled=11539 (accessed February 14, 2008).

[12] Slavin, 209.

[13] Slavin, 214.

into the international community or progressively stronger political and economic sanctions. She also highlighted that the new U.S. position was more of a gesture to the members of the UN Security Council and Germany than to Iran. "In agreeing to talk to Iran with preconditions and chaperones, the Bush administration was holding its nose while it stretched out a pinky toward Tehran—the same strategy that failed to stop North Korea's march toward becoming a nuclear weapons state."[14] Time and time again, the administration demonstrated its difficulty in meeting a fundamental requirement of negotiating success—showing a modicum of respect for your adversary. [15] The administration's handling of Iran seems more likely to evolve into war with Iran before Bush leaves office, but a bi-partisan panel's recommendation of opening talks makes military confrontation no longer likely.[16] Additionally, current situations in Afghanistan and Iraq make such confrontation improbable as well.

Active Engagement with Iran

Many analysts, policy experts, and prominent members of Western and Persian societies agree that both the U.S. and the Islamic Republic of Iran should immediately capitalize on open and unlimited dialogue with each other, particularly at the most senior levels. This would represent a significant U.S. policy shift, which presented itself at opportune times after the September 11 attacks but never received attention. For this dramatic policy shift to be realistic and appealing to both the U.S. and Iran, initial dialogue on topics of significant interest which are also non-controversial helps to create

---

[14] Slavin, 223.

[15] Slavin, 222.

[16] Slavin, 225.

positive momentum to tackle the more difficult issues. The talks presented by Iranian diplomats in 2003 that never materialized were possibly too all-encompassing. Nevertheless, there exist issues that have the potential to be resolved with relative ease. An examination of the current administration's lack of communication with the Islamic Republic reveals that the U.S. and Iran were basically on the same team in combating al-Qaeda and the Taliban. Additionally, results from investigations on Iran's nuclear weapons development program, while some Americans may argue are misleading, give Iran legitimate grounds to continue its research in nuclear energy development.

Starting Points

Bilateral engagements are critical components for U.S.-Iran relations. However, U.S. foreign policy with Iran becomes even more effective when the policy integration occurs at the international level. Overwhelming consensus in forums that organizations like the United Nations offer creates a unified international community which addresses relevant issues of world-wide concern. Human suffering, Global War on Terror and Proliferation are examples of undeniable topics that the international community does not object to addressing, particularly when irrefutable evidence exists. So long as the U.S. is able to define policies within broad areas such as these, its approach will remain internationally acceptable and effective.

This paper recommends that the U.S. reinvigorate the collaboration that existed in the early years of Operation Enduring Freedom (OEF), when U.S. and Iranian diplomats secretly discussed how to best deal with the Taliban and al-Qaeda, but in an open venue. Such a gesture not only recognizes the strategic importance of Iran in the American struggle against Taliban and al-Qaeda but it also suggests that the Axis of Evil metaphor no longer applies to the Islamic Republic. Since al-Qaeda is threatens Iran from two fronts, Afghanistan and Iraq, there is even potential for Iran to assist the U.S.in dealing with al-Qaeda in Iraq (AIQ). The U.S. ought to show appreciation for any Iranian cooperation in efforts to capture and prosecute their mutual enemies by providing U.S. cooperation with regards to the MEK in Iraq, along with formally renouncing the Islamic Republic as a member of the Axis of Evil.

With the nuclear issue, international skepticism resulting from a recent National Intelligence Estimate (NIE) on the nuclear intentions and capabilities of Iran has created some doubt amongst nations, shifting the balance in favor of Iran. From the Office of the U.S. Director of National Intelligence (DNI):

> We judge with high confidence that in fall 2003, Tehran halted its nuclear weapons program; we also assess with moderate-to-high confidence that Tehran at a minimum is keeping open the option to develop nuclear weapons. We judge with high confidence that the halt, and Tehran's announcement of its decision to suspend its declared uranium enrichment program and sign an Additional Protocol to is Nuclear Non-Proliferation Treaty Safeguards Agreement, was directed primarily in response to increasing international scrutiny and pressure resulting from exposure of Iran's previously undeclared nuclear work.[17]

While the NIE still leaves room for the possibility of nuclear weapons development, the most defining aspect in the report is that Tehran halted its weapons program, raising the question of the need for UN Security Council Resolutions and sanctions. Suspicions without confirmation from evidence are not acceptable internationally, especially since the U.S. made a costly mistake in the Iraq invasion, when extensive searches produced no active WMD programs, which the U.S. believed Saddam Hussein possessed.

---

[17] National Intelligence Council, 6.

In order to see progress with Iran regarding the nuclear issue, the U.S. ought to lead the UN in reversing its current initiatives. Nations presented a third draft resolution to the UN Security Council despite a lack of evidence:

> Compared with the two previous UN Security Council resolutions on Iran, the new draft will include travel restrictions and bans for more Iranian; an expansion of asset freezes; curbs on dual-us items and export credit; financial monitoring; cargo inspections on aircraft and vessels; and possible "next steps." Analysts say the new draft was basically following the modalities of Resolutions 1737 and 1747 with the aim of imposing appropriate pressure on Tehran to provide impetus for a diplomatic solution to the Iranian nuclear issue.[18]

While the five permanent members of the UN Security Council have reached broad consensus over the draft resolution, "the U.S. and other Western Security Council members want the resolution to clear the council unanimously so as to signify the solidarity of the international community," but "some of the ten non-permanent members, like South Africa, Indonesia, and Libya, have already raised objections or doubts over the resolution." [19] Since negative support for the resolution does reside with some members, the U.S. would not be a lone voice, so an American objection to the necessity of a new resolution would strategically communicate to all that it is time to trust Iran again.

The U.S. under President Ronald W. Reagan faced a formidable adversary in the Soviet Union, but through his diplomatic efforts, he eventually led the free world in watching the Communism in Eastern Europe fall. Rather than isolating the Soviet Union, President Reagan sought to trust the adversary but verify:

> What it all boils down to is this. I want the new closeness to continue. And it will, as long as we make it clear that we will continue to act in a certain way as

---

[18] Campaign Against Sanctions and Military Intervention in Iran, "Iran faces fresh pressure from UN Security Council," 27 Feb 2008, under "Stronger Sanctions," http://www.campaigniran.org/casmii/index.php?q=node/4175 (accessed March 1, 2008).

[19] Campaign Against Sanctions and Military Intervention in Iran, "Iran faces fresh pressure from UN Security Council."

long as they continue to act in a helpful manner. If and when they don't, at first pull your punches. If they persist, pull the plug. It's still trust but verify. It's still play, but cut the cards. It's still watch closely. And don't be afraid to see what you see.[20]

The U.S. and the international community should adopt this approach that Reagan advocates. Lifting sanctions and increasing dialogue, while simultaneously monitoring Iran's nuclear activities will benefit all those involved. If or when oversight reveals a new reality, the U.S. ought to continue the dialogue until resolutions occur or more aggressive measure are warranted.

Beyond the dialogue amongst the senior leadership, steps to encourage greater people-to-people contact will foster better understanding between the two nations:

> People-to-people exchanges, especially on non-political issues such as medicine and the environment, can help cultivate a more informed policy community and enhance individual and institutional incentives for normalization. In addition, the State Department should consider licensing non-governmental organizations to operate in Iran, which would obviate the need for multiple waivers and facilitate greater interaction. The administration should also improve Iranian students' access to American high education institutions by improving links, reintroducing standardized tests, and facilitating student visas.[21]

Saudi-U.S. Policy Non-Integration

The Bush administration seeks a unified effort in the Middle East but continues to meet mixed emotions from different states. His visit to the region in January 2008 to address the many security issues did little to galvanize support. "Analysts say Bush got a mixed response from Arab leaders on his three top issues: He received encouragement in

---

[20] Ronald W. Reagan, "Farewell Address to the Nation" (January 11, 1989), http://www.reaganfoundation.org/reagan/speeches/farewell.asp (accessed February 13, 2008)

[21] Suazanne Maloney, "America and Iran: From Containment to Coexistence" *Brookings Policy Brief* no. 87 (August 2001), under "Six Preliminary Steps for the Bush Administration," http://www.brookings.edu/~/media/Files/rc/papers/2001/08iran_maloney/pb87.pdf (accessed March 1, 2008).

promoting Arab-Israeli peace, he was ignored on the expansion of democratic rights, and he was firmly rebuffed on confronting Iran."[22]

Repercussions for Saudi alignment with the U.S. in its handling of Iran have the potential to be too grave for the Kingdom and the U.S. Unity with an infidel that toppled another Muslim state is an image Saudi Arabia does not wish to portray, and the U.S. must be sensitive to a Middle East opinion that is very cautious of collaboration with a Western power. Saudi foreign policy with Iran is best suited when the range of those involved remain at the regional level. Non-integration with the U.S. enables the Kingdom to affect the Sunni-Shiite tension without creating the impression that the U.S. favors a particular sect; and within an Arab and Persian context, discussions, debates, and even arguments tend to run smoother. While this paper advocates that the U.S. distance itself from particular regional issues such as the Sunni-Shiite divide, the U.S. must remain observant of the progress that may or may not develop. Recent trends of continuous, relatively open dialogue between Saudi Arabia and Iran ought to encourage the U.S. to remain on the sidelines.

---

[22] Borzou Daragahi, "Bush fails to persuade Arab allies," *Los Angeles Times,* January 19, 2008, http://www.latimes.com/new/printedition/asection/la-fg-iran19jan19,5232944,print.stor (accessed January 31, 2008).

Chapter Nine

9. CONCLUSION

With the invasion of Iraq in 2003 and its subsequent instability, the Kingdom of Saudi Arabia and the Islamic Republic of Iran find themselves at the center of a struggle for power in the Middle East. The Sunni-dominant Kingdom, with its oil wealth, religious and cultural importance, and Arab voice, competes in a battle to increase soft power influence against the Shiite-dominant Islamic Republic, a nation strengthened with the collapse of the Hussein regime that seeks to regain its empirical past.

Recent history between the two regional powers reveals that balancing the Sunni and Shiite influence has always been a concern between this Arab and Persian nation. Now, the Islamic Republic seeks to build its power base through lending support to particular factions in regional struggles; groups like HAMAS and Hezbollah, although not tied culturally to Iran, welcomes the Islamic Republic coming to their aid, as they struggle for survival. Additionally, others argue that Iran is pursuing a nuclear weapons capability not only to deter aggressors but to gain status in the international community. In response to these behaviors, Saudi Arabia remains actively engaged in the region to counterbalance the potential growth of Iranian influence. The Arab Peace Initiate, or King Abdullah's Plan, seeks to bring a conclusion to the Arab-Israeli conflict. This initiative, spearheaded with all of the kingdom's weight and importance behind it, negates the need for HAMAS and Hezbollah to receive support from Iran. In response to aggressive behavior against Sunni populations such as in Iraq, the Saudi approach entails lending direct support to Sunni factions.

Beyond the practical and diplomatic approach to managing the crises just described, King Abdullah of Saudi Arabia employs direct and indirect methods in dealing with Iran. Through Arab organizations such as the GCC, the Kingdom subtly reminds Iran of the effect of Arab unity. The GCC acts as a vehicle by which a regional union of Arab nations can indirectly influence Iran through military programs such as Peninsula Shield and economic programs such as the Gulf Common Market. Most importantly, Saudi Arabian leadership complements these indirect acts by maintaining an open and respectful dialogue with the Islamic Republic's senior officials.

The Saudi approach sharply contrasts with present U.S. foreign policy with Iran. As opposed to viewing Iran as an equal, the Bush administration imposed the Axis of Evil label on Iran which will continue to incite Iranian contempt and motivate non-compliant behavior. The Bush administration's isolation of Iran, the surviving component of Clinton's dual containment policy, utilizes unilateral and multilateral restrictions on the Islamic Republic in order to affect its behavior. Because of the nuclear issue, measures such as sanctions are growing in intensity. The majority of the senior officials of the Bush administration failed and continues to fail to recognize strategic opportunities that may bring resolution to Iranian issues. Although Iran quietly cooperated during the early stages of OEF, the U.S. chose not to recognize Iran's assistance as an opportunity to foster better relations with the Islamic Republic. The President and members of his cabinet, such as Cheney and Rumsfeld, prefers to further alienate Iran from the U.S. and seeks to gain increased support of this type of behavior from the international community. Iran overcomes U.S. sanctions effectively in a global economy and the international community remains divided over issues with Iran. Despite the isolation efforts, Iran resists to cooperate, calling into question the validity of Bush approach.

This thesis identifies the appropriateness of the Saudi approach to handling Iran from a regional perspective. The Kingdom understands the ethnic, cultural, and religious dimension with which it must justify its actions, and it recognizes that the issues must be resolved through dialogue. This thesis challenges the relevancy of the current U.S. foreign policy, advocating instead alternative unilateral and multilateral efforts. The U.S., Iran, and the international community share a common enemy in the form of al-Qaeda and this is easily a good and non-controversial topic for the U.S. to begin the open dialogue with Iran. This thesis also suggests the importance of the U.S. retracting the Axis of Evil label from the Islamic Republic, and recommends pursuing dialogue that initially encompasses critical, internationally recognized issues in world forums with senior Iranian leadership such as the Global War on Terror and Proliferation. To be effective, both Saudi and U.S. approaches should remain separate—one that is regionally acceptable and one that is internationally legitimate.

While the motivations of the U.S. and the Kingdom may differ, their dissimilar methods to reduce the influence of Iran are necessary. Two pillars of effort, one at the international level headed by the U.S. and one at the regional level executed by Saudi Arabia, both acting independently, may effectively marginalize Iran as a threat.

BIBLIOGRAPHY

Aarts, Paul and Gerd Nonneman. *Saudi Arabia in the Balance: Political Economy, Society, Foreign Affairs.* New York: New York University Press, 2005.

Aburish, Said K. *The Rise, Corruption and Coming Fall of the House of Saud.* New York: St. Martin's/Griffin, 2003.

Agence France-Presse, "Bush seen facing difficult talks during Riyadh visit." *Gulf Times,* January 14, 2008. http://www.gulf-times.com/site/topics/article.asp?cu_no=2&item_no=195586&version=1&template_id=37&parent_id=17 (accessed 31 Jan 2008).

Agencies. "Iran and Saudi pledge friendship." *Al Jazeera.* March 3, 2007. http://english.aljazeera.net/NR/exeres/D4EEF783-C1CE-467F-824C-DD67943B2255.htm (accessed February 15, 2008).

Ahrari, M.E. *The Gulf and International Security: The 1980s and Beyond.* New York: St Martin's Press, 1989.

Al-Hattlan, Sulaiman. "In Saudi Arabia, an Extreme Problem." *Washington Post*, May 8, 2002.

Ambah, Faiza Saleh Ambah. "Many Arabs Applaud Hezbollah." *The Washington Post,* May 11, 2007.

Amuzegar, Jahangir. "The Ahmadinejad Era: Preparing for the Apocalypse." *Journal of International Affairs* 60, no.2 (Spring/Summer 2007): 35-53.

Armanios, Febe. "Islam: Sunnis and Shiite." Congressional Research Service. February 23, 2005.

Associated Press. "Khamenei reverses gas cut decision by Ahmadinejad." *Gulf News.* January 21, 2008. http://archive.gulfnews.com/articles/08/01/22/10183770.html (accessed February 28, 2008).

Associated Press. "Six Arab Gulf states to announce common market in December." *International Herald Tribune,* October 10, 2007. http://www.iht.com/articles/ap/2007/10/10/business/ME-GEN-Gulf-Common-Market.php (accessed January 31, 2008).

Bahgat, Gawdat. "Saudi Arabia and the Arab-Israeli Peace Process." *Middle East Policy* XIV, no. 3 (2007): 49-59.

British Petroleum (BP). *Statistical Review of World Energy,* June 2005. http://www.bp.com/liveassets/bp_internet/switzerland/corporate_switzerland/STAGING/local_assets/downloads_pdfs/s/statistical_review_of_world_energy_2005.pdf (accessed January 31, 2008).

Bronson, Rachel. *Thicker Than Oil—America's Uneasy Partnership with Saudi Arabia—America's Uneasy Partnership with Saudi Arabia.* New York: Oxford University Press, 2006.

Brown, Anthony Cave. *Oil, God, and Gold: The Story of Aramco and the Saudi Kings.* Boston: Houghton Mifflin, 1999.

Bush, George W. Office of the President of the United States. "State of the Union Address." January 29, 2002. http://www.whitehouse.gov/new/releases/2002/01/20020129-11.htm (accessed February 15, 2008).

---. Office of the President of the United States. *National Security Strategy of the United States of America.* March 16, 2006.

Campaign Against Sanctions and Military Intervention in Iran. "Iran faces fresh pressure from UN Security Council." 27 Feb 2008. http://www.campaigniran.org/casmii/index.php?q=node/4175 (accessed March 1, 2008).

Cooper, Helene. "After the Mecca Accord, Clouded Horizons." *The New York Times,* July 17, 2006.

Cordesman, Anthony H. *Iran's Developing Military Capabilities.* Washington, D.C.: Center for Strategic and International Studies, 2005.

---. *The Military Balance in the Middle East.* Westport, Connecticut: Praeger Publishers, 2004.

Cordesman, Anthony H. and Khalid R. Al-Rodhan. *Gulf Military Forces in an Era of Asymmetric War.* Westport, Connecticut: Praeger Security International, 2007.

Cordesman, Anthony H. Cordesman and Martin Kleiber. *Iran's Military Forces and Warfighting Capabilities.* Westport, Connecticut: Praeger Security International, 2007.

Cottam, R.W. "Charting Iran's New Course." *Current History,* 90, no. 1 (1991): 21-37.

Daragahi, Borzou. "Bush fails to persuade Arab allies." *Los Angeles Times,* January 19, 2008. http://www.latimes.com/new/printedition/asection/la-fg-iran19jan19,5232944,print.stor (accessed January 31, 2008).

Dobbins, James. "My Enemy's Enemy." RAND Corporation. February 27, 2007. http://www.rand.org/commentary/022707IHT.html (accessed February 13, 2008).

---. "Time to Deal with Iran." *Washington Post.* May 6, 2004.

Freedman, Robert O. *The Middle East Enters the Twenty-First Century.* Gainesville, Florida: University Press of Florida, 2002.

Fürtig, Henner. *Iran's Rivalry with Saudi Arabia Between the Gulf Wars.* United Kingdom: Garnet Publishing Limited, 2002.

G8. Kananaskis Summit -2002. "The G8 global partnership against the spread of weapons and materials of mass destruction." 2002. http://www.g8.fr/evian/english/navigation/g8_documents/archives_from_...agains t_the_spread_of_weapns_and _materials_of_mass_destruction.html (accessed February 12, 2008).

Gause, F. Gregory III. "Saudi Arabia: Iraq, Iran, the Regional Power Balance, and the Sectarian Question." *Strategic Insights,* VI, no. 2 (March 2007): 1-8. http://www.ccc.nps.navy.mil/si/2007/Mar/gauseMar07.pdf (accessed January 10, 2008).

Ghafour, P.K. Abdul. "GCC Common Market Becomes a Reality." *Arab News,* January 1, 2008. http://www.arabnews.com/?page=1&section=0&article=105173&d=1&m=1&y= 2008 (accessed January 31, 2008).

Heradstveit, Daniel and G. Matthew Bonham. "What the Axis of Evil Metaphor Did to Iran." *The Middle East Journal*, 61, no. 3 (Summer 2007): 421-440.

Hunter, Robert E. "Time to Talk to Iran." RAND Corporation. April 26, 2006. http://www.rand.org/commentary/042606WP.html (accessed February 13, 2008).

---. "Grand Strategy for the Middle East." RAND Corporation. November 19, 2006. http://www.rand.org/commentary/111906SDUT.html (accessed February 13, 2008).

Indyk, Martin, Graham Fuller, Anthony H. Cordesman, and Phebe Marr. "Symposium on Dual Containment: U.S. Policy Toward Iran and Iraq. *Middle East Policy* 3, no. 1 (1994): 1-26.

International Monetary Fund. Islamic Republic of Iran: Statistical Appendix. IMF Country Report 04/307. Washington, D.C.: International Monetary Fund, 2004.

Ira, Kumaran. "France obtains energy deals, establishes first military base in Persian Gulf." World Socialist Web Site. http://www.wewe.org/articles/2008/jan2008/sark-j24.shtml (accessed February 15, 2008)

Islamic Republic News Agency. "Iran-Saudi Arabian parliamentary friendship group hold meeting in Riyadh." January 27, 2008. http://www2.irna.ir/en/news/view/menu-234/0801271690004753.htm (accessed 15 Feb 2008).

Joseph, Robert G. Office of the Under Secretary for Arms Control and International Security. "The Bush Administration Approach to Combating the Proliferation of Weapons of Mass Destruction." Remarks, Carnegie International Nonproliferation Conference, Washington, DC, November 7, 2005. http://www.state.gov/t/us/rm/56584.htm (accessed February 10, 2008).

Kahwaji, Riad. "GCC Creates Quick-Reaction Force." *Defense News,* February 4, 2008.

Kessler, Glenn Kessler. "In 2003, U.S. Spurned Iran's Offer of Dialogue." *The Washington Post,* June 18, 2006. http://www.washingtonpost.com/wp-dyn/content/article/2006/06/17/AR006061700727_pf.html (accessed February 29, 2008).

Khan, M. Ghazanfar Ali. "GCC to Discuss 'Peninsula Shield' Expansion." *Arab News.* November 2, 2006. http://www.arabnews.com/?page=4&section=0&article=83184&d=2&m=11&y=2006 (accessed February 13, 2008).

Kingdom of Saudi Arabia. Ministry of Foreign Affairs. "Kingdom Foreign Policy— The foreign policy of the Kingdom of Saudi Arabia." http://www.mofa.gov.sa/Detail.asp?InSectionID=3989&InNewsItemID=34645 (accessed February 14, 2008).

Kissinger, Henry. "Reflections on Containment." *Foreign Affairs*, 73, No. 3 (May/June 1994): 113-130. http://ezproxy6.ndu.edu/login?url=http://search.ebscohost.com/login.aspx?direct=true&db=afh&AN=9409082432&site=ehost-live (accessed February 14, 2008).

Lakoff, George and Mark Johnson. *Metaphors We Live By.* Chicago: University of Chicago Press, 1980.

Maloney, Suzanne. "America and Iran: From Containment to Coexistence." *Brookings Policy Brief* no. 87 (August 2001). http://www.brookings.edu/~/media/Files/rc/papers/2001/08iran_maloney/pb87.pdf (accessed March 1, 2008).

Middle East Economic Digest. "Gaining Confidence." *Middle East Economic Digest* 51, no. 7 (February 16, 2007): 41-43. http://ezproxy6.ndu.edu/login?url=http://search.ebscohost.com/login.aspx?direct= true&db=bsh&AN=24360442&site=ehost-live (accessed October 24, 2007).

Mraz, Jerr L. and John P. McCallen. "Dual Containment in the Persian Gulf: Strategic Considerations and Policy Options." master's thesis, Naval Postgraduate School, 1996. http://stinet.dtic.mil/cgi-bin/GetTRDoc?AD=ADA311402&Location=U2$doc=GetTRDoc.pdf (accessed February 16, 2008).

National Intelligence Council. *National Intelligence Estimate – Iran: Nuclear Intentions and Capabilities.* Prepared by the Office of the Director of National Intelligence. November 2007. http://www.dni.gov/press_releases/200712013_release.pdf (accessed March 1, 2008).

Obaid, Nawaf. *Saudi Arabia's Strategic Energy Initiative: Safeguarding Against Supply Disruptions.* Riyadh, Saudi Arabia: Saudi National Security Assessment Project, 2006. http://www.saudi-us-relations.org/fact-book/documents/2006/060904-snsap-energy-initiative.pdf (accessed January 31, 2008).

---. "Stepping Into Iraq." *The Washington Post.* November 29, 2006.

Office of the Press Secretary. "US Eases Economic Embargo Against Libya." April 23, 2004. http://www.whitehouse.gov/news/releases/2004/04/print/20040423-9.html (accessed February 13, 2008).

Organization of the Petroleum Exporting Countries. "Who are OPEC Member Countries?" Organization of the Petroleum Exporting Countries. http://www.opec.org/library/FAQs/aboutOPEC/q3.htm (accessed January 27, 2008).

Ottaway, David B. "U.S. Eyes Money Trails of Saudi-Backed Charities." *Washington Post*, August 19, 2004.

Pan, Esther and Jayshree Bajoria. "The U.S.-India Nuclear Deal." Council on Foreign Relations. February 7, 2008. http://www.cfr.org/publication/9663/ (accessed February 13, 2008).

Peterson, J.E. "Saudi Arabia and the Illusion of Security." *Adelphi Paper 348* (July 2002): 7.

Pollack, Kenneth M. *The Persian Puzzle: The Conflict Between Iran and America.* New York: Random House, 2004.

Porter, Gareth. "How a 2003 secret overture from Tehran might have led to a deal on Iran's nuclear capacity—if the Bush administration hadn't rebuffed it." *The American Prospect.* May 21, 2006. http://www.prospect.org/cs/articles?articled=11539 (accessed February 14, 2008).

Posner, Gerald. *Secrets of the Kingdom.* New York: Random House, 2005.

Reagan, Ronald W. Office of the President of the United States. "Farewell Address to the Nation." January 11, 1989. http://www.reaganfoundation.org/reagan/speeches/farewell.asp (accessed February 13, 2008).

Regan, Tom. "Report: Cheney Rejected Iran's Offer of Concessions in 2003." *The Christian Science Monitor- csmonitor.com*, January 18, 2007. http://www.csmonitor.com/2007/0118/p99s01-duts.html (accessed February 15, 2008).

Ricoeur, Paul. *Rule of Metaphor.* Toronto: University of Toronto Press, 1977.

Rosen, Nir. "The Flight From Iraq." *The New York Times.* May 13, 2007. http://www.nytimes.com/2007/05/13/magazine/13refugees-t.html?pagewanted=10&r=1&fta=y (accessed February 13, 2008).

The Royal Embassy of Saudi Arabia. "The Arab Peace Initiative." *Middle East Policy* IX, no. 2 (June 2007): 25-26.

Slavin, Barbara. *Bitter Friends, Bosom Enemies—Iran, the U.S. and the Twisted Path to Confrontation.* New York: St. Martin's Press, 2007.

Smith, Dan. *The State of the Middle East.* Los Angeles, California: University of California Press, 2006.

Stern, Roger. "The Iranian Petroleum Crisis and United States National Security." *Proceeding of the National Academy of Sciences* 104, no. 1377 (January 2, 2007). http://www.ncbi.nlm.nih.gov/pubmed/17190820 (accessed January 31, 2008).

Strategic Forecasting, Inc. "Iran: An Invitation to the Gulf Cooperation Council." November 29, 2007. http://www.stratfor.com/analysis/iran_invitation_gulf_cooperation_council (accessed February 15, 2008).

Tahir, Khudayr. "Did the Iraqi Satellite Channel spy on Abu Rishah." British *Broadcasting Corporation Worldwide Monitoring.* September 16, 2007. http://www.lexisnexis.com/us/Inacademic/results/docview/docview.do?risb=21_T 3196545951&format=GNBF&sort=RELEVANCE&startDocNo=1&resultsUrlKe

y=29_T3196545956&cisb=22_T3196545955&treeMax=true&treeWidth=0&csi=
10962&docNo=1 (accessed February 13, 2008).

"U.S. Consultancy Claims Iran Has Built Underground Missile Factories." *Jane's
Missiles and Rockets,* December 8, 2005.

U.S. Department of Energy. Energy Information Administration. *Country Energy
Profiles,* 2006. http://tonto.eia.doe.gov/country/index.cfm (accessed March 6,
2008).

U.S. Department of State. Bureau of Near Eastern Affairs. *Background Note: Saudi
Arabia,* February 2008. http://www.state.gov/r/pa/ei/bgn/3584.htm (accessed
January 6, 2008).

U.S. Department of State. Bureau of Verification and Compliance. *World Military
Expenditures and Arms Transfers 1999-2000.*
http://www.fas.org/man/docs/wmeat9900/index.html (accessed January 31, 2008)

U.S. Government Accountability Office. "Iran Sanctions—Impact in Furthering U.S.
Objectives Is Unclear and Should Be Reviewed." *Report to the Ranking Member,
Subcommittee on National Security and Foreign Affairs, House Committee on
Oversight and Government Reform.* December 2007. Washington, DC:
Government Printing Office, 2007. http://www.gao.gov/highlights/d0858high.pdf
(accessed February 10, 2008).

Vick, Charles P. "Weapons of Mass Destruction- Shahab-3, 3A/Zelzal-3."
GlobalSecurity.org, February 15, 2007.
http://www.globalsecurity.org/wmd/world/iran/shahab-3.htm (accessed March 5,
2008).

Wilson, Isaiah III. "Rediscovering Containment: The Sources of American-Iranian
Conduct." *Journal of International Affairs* 60, no. 2 (Spring/Summer 2007): 95-
112.

Zarif, Mohammad Javad. "Tackling the U.S.-Iran Crisis: The Need for a Paradigm Shift."
Journal of International Affairs 60, no. 2 (Spring/Summer 2007): 73-94.

About the Author

Major Romeo R. Macalintal Jr., is a New Jersey native. As a graduate of the United States Military Academy at West Point, he earned a Bachelor's of Science degree in Engineering Management as a Second Lieutenant in 1995 in the branch of Aviation. After completion of Initial Entry Rotary Wing and Officer Basic School and OH-58D Kiowa Warrior aircraft qualification at Fort Rucker, Alabama and , he had an initial assignment to the 101st Airborne Division at Fort Campbell, Kentucky. In his first operational assignment, MAJ Macalintal served as the Platoon Leader, Squadron Assistant Logistics Officer and Squadron Adjutant for the 2nd Squadron, 17th Cavalry Regiment, and Company Executive Officer for Charlie Company, 1st Battalion, 58th Aviation Regiment (Air Traffic Services).

In the winter of 1999, MAJ Macalintal attended the Military Intelligence Officer Transition Course, followed by the Military Intelligence Captain's Career Course at Fort Huachuca, Arizona. With subsequent assignment to the 82nd Airborne Division at Fort Bragg, North Carolina, he served as the Brigade Training Officer and Brigade Operations Officer prior to assuming command of the Headquarters Company, 82nd Aviation Brigade for 22 months, which included a tour Operation Enduring Freedom combat tour in Afghanistan from 2002 to 2003. Upon completion of this command, MAJ Macalintal assumed command of Alpha Company, 1st Battalion, 82nd Aviation Regiment, a flight company that would deploy in support of Operation Iraqi Freedom from 2003 to 2004.

MAJ Macalintal proceeded to his next assignment to Fort Dix, New Jersey as an Active Component/Reserve Component Aviation Team Chief for the 78th Division. MAJ Macalintal redeployed to the Central Command Area of Responsibility to serve as the United States Training Mission to Saudi Arabia's Aviation Advisor to the Royal Saudi Land Forces Aviation Corps Commander. He proceeded to his current assignment as a student of the Joint Forces Staff College's Joint Advanced Warfighting School.

MAJ Macalintal's awards and decorations include the Bronze Star, the Joint Meritorious Unit Award, the Meritorious Service Medal, the Air Medal, the Joint Commendation Medal, the Army Commendation Medal, the Army Achievement Medal, the Iraq Campaign Medal, the Afghanistan Campaign Medal, the National Defense Service Medal, the Combat Action Badge, the Army Aviator Badge, the Senior Parachutist Badge, the Air Assault Badge, and the German Parachutist Badge.

MAJ Macalintal is married to the former Melissa Knotts of Troy, Alabama. They have four children: Tyler, Kaitlyn, Rachel, and Samantha.